MW00779741

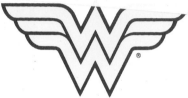

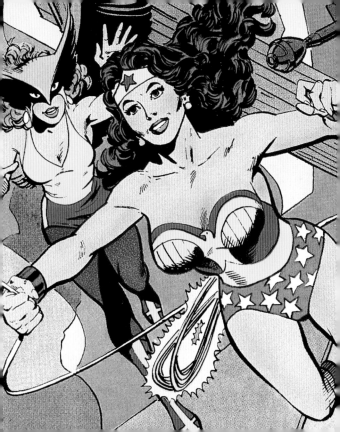

WONDER WOMAN

Introduction by GLORIA STEINEM

FEATURING OVER FIVE DECADES OF GREAT COVERS

A Tiny Folio™

ABBEVILLE PRESS • PUBLISHERS
NEW YORK • LONDON • PARIS

Front cover: Detail of *Wonder Woman* (Second Series) 63
Back cover: *Wonder Woman* (First Series) 1
Frontispiece: Detail of *Wonder Woman* (First Series) 249

Editors: Amy Handy (Abbeville) and Steven Korté (DC Comics)
Production editor: Owen Dugan
Designer: Molly Shields
Production supervisor: Lou Bilka

First edition
10 9 8 7 6 5 4 3 2 1

Wonder Woman created by William Moulton Marston.

A portion of the text by Gloria Steinem appeared in *Wonder Woman*, a *Ms.* Book
published by Holt, Rinehart and Winston, Inc., and Warner Books, Inc., 1972.

The captions note the pencil and ink artists for each cover as could best be determined.
While the authors have endeavored to identify all of the artists involved, they apologize
to any person not identified and invite such person to inform them of the error.

Library of Congress Cataloging-in-Publication Data
Wonder Woman : featuring over five decades of great covers /
    introduction by Gloria Steinem.
        p.   cm.
    Includes index.
    ISBN 0-7892-0012-0
PN6727.W6W6   1995
741.5'973—dc20   94-23837

INTRODUCTION
by Gloria Steinem

Wonder Woman is the only female super-hero to be published continuously since comic books began—indeed, she is one of the few to have existed at all or to be anything other than part of a male super-hero group—but this may strike many readers as a difference without much distinction. After all, haven't comic books always been a little disreputable? Something that would never have been assigned in school? The answer to those questions is yes, which is exactly why they are important. Comic books have power—including over the child who still lives within each of us—because they are *not* part of the "serious" grown-up world.

I remember hundreds of nights reading comic books under the covers with a flashlight; dozens of car trips while my parents told me I was ruining my eyes and perhaps my mind ("brain-deadeners" was what my mother called them); and countless hours spent hiding in a tree or some other inaccessible spot where I could pore over their pages in sweet freedom. Because my family's traveling meant I didn't go to school regularly until I was about twelve, comic books joined cereal boxes and ketchup labels as the primers that taught me how to read. They were even cheap enough to be the first things I bought on my own—a customer who couldn't see over the countertop but whose dignity was greatly enhanced by making a choice, counting out carefully hoarded coins, and completing a grown-up exchange.

I've always wondered if this seemingly innate drive toward independence in children isn't more than just "a movement toward mastery," as psychologists say. After all, each of us is the result of millennia of environment and heredity, a unique combination that could never happen before—or again. Like a seed that contains a plant, a child is already a unique person; an ancient spirit born into a body too small to express itself, or even cope with the world. I remember feeling the greatest love for my parents whenever they allowed me to express my own will, whether that meant wearing an inappropriate hat for days on end, or eating dessert before I had finished dinner.

Perhaps it's our memories of past competence and dreams for the future that create the need for super-heroes in the first place. Leaping skyscrapers in a single bound, seeing through walls, and forcing people to tell the truth by encircling them in a magic lasso—all would be satisfying fantasies at any age, but they may be psychological necessities when we have trouble tying our shoes, escaping a worldview composed mainly of belts and knees, and getting grown-ups to *pay attention*.

The problem is that the super-heroes who perform magical feats—indeed, even mortal heroes who are merely competent—are almost always men. A female child is left to believe that, even when her body is as big as her spirit, she will still be helping with minor tasks, appreciating the accomplishments of others, and waiting to be rescued. Of course, pleasure is to be found in all these experiences of helping, appreciating, and being rescued; pleasure that should be open to boys, too. Even in comic books, heroes sometimes work in groups or are called upon to protect their own kind, not just helpless females. But the truth is that a male super-hero is more likely to be vulnerable, if only to create suspense, than a female character is to be powerful or independent. For little girls, the only alternative is suppressing a crucial part of ourselves by transplanting our consciousness into a male character—which usually means a white one, thus penalizing girls of color doubly, and boys of color, too. Otherwise, choices remain limited: in the case of girls, to an "ideal" life of sitting around like a Technicolor clotheshorse, getting into jams with villains, and saying things like, "Oh, Superman! I'll always be grateful to you"; in the case of boys of color, to identifying with villains who may be the only ethnic characters with any power; and in the case of girls of color, to making an impossible choice between parts of their identity. It hardly seems worth learning to tie our shoes.

I'm happy to say that I was rescued from this dependent fate at the age of seven or so; rescued (Great Hera!) by a woman. Not only did she have the wisdom of Athena and Aphrodite's power to inspire love, she was also faster than Mercury and stronger than Hercules. In her all-woman home on Paradise Island, a refuge of ancient Amazon culture protected from nosy travelers by magnetic thought-fields that created an area known to the world as the Bermuda Triangle, she had come to her many and amazing powers naturally. Together with her Amazon sisters, she had been trained in them from infancy and perfected them in Greek-style contests of dexterity, strength, and speed. The lesson was that each of us might have unknown powers within us, if we only believed and practiced them. (To me, it always seemed boring that Superman had bulletproof skin, X-ray vision, and the ability to fly. Where was the contest?) Though definitely white, as were all her Amazon sisters, she was tall and strong, with dark hair and eyes—a relief from the weak, bosomy, blonde heroines of the 1940s.

Of course, this Amazon did need a few fantastic gadgets to help her once she entered a modern world governed by Ares, God of War, not Aphrodite, Goddess of Love: a magic golden lasso that compelled all within its coils to obey her command, silver bracelets that repelled bullets, and an invisible plane that carried her through time as well as space. But she still had to learn how to throw the lasso with accuracy, be agile enough to deflect bullets from her silver-encased wrists, and navigate an invisible plane.

Charles Moulton, whose name appeared on each episode as Wonder Woman's writer and creator, had seen straight into my heart and understood the fears of violence and humiliation hidden there. No longer did I have to pretend to like the "POW!" and "SPLAT!" of boys' comic books, from Captain Marvel to the Green Hornet. No longer did I have nightmares after looking at ghoulish images of torture and murder, bloody scenes made all the more realistic by steel-booted Nazis and fang-toothed Japanese who were caricatures of World War II enemies then marching in every newsreel. (Eventually, the sadism of boys' comic books was so extreme that it inspired Congressional hearings, and publishers were asked to limit the number of severed heads and dripping entrails—a reminder that television wasn't the first popular medium selling sadism to boys.) Best of all, I could stop pretending to enjoy the ridicule, bossing-around, and constant endangering of female characters. In these Amazon adventures, only the villains bought the idea that "masculine" meant aggression and "feminine" meant submission. Only the occasional female accomplice said things like "Girls want superior men to boss them around," and even they were usually converted to the joys of self-respect by the story's end.

This was an Amazon super-hero who never killed her enemies. Instead, she converted them to a belief in equality and peace, to self-reliance, and respect for the rights of others. If villains destroyed themselves, it was through their own actions or some unbloody accident. Otherwise, they might be conquered by force, but it was a force tempered by love and justice.

In short, she was wise, beautiful, brave, and explicitly out to change "a world torn by the hatreds and wars of men."

She was Wonder Woman.

Only much later, when I was in my thirties and modern feminism had begun to explain the political roots of women's status—instead of accepting some "natural" inferiority decreed by biology, God, or Freud—did I realize how hard Charles Moulton had tried to get an egalitarian worldview into comic book form. From Wonder Woman's birth myth as Princess Diana of Paradise Island, "that enlightened land," to her adventures in America disguised as Diana Prince, a bespectacled army nurse and intelligence officer (a clear steal from Superman's Clark Kent), this female super-hero was devoted to democracy, peace, justice, and "liberty and freedom for all womankind."

One typical story centers on Prudence, a young pioneer in the days of the American Frontier, where Wonder Woman has been transported by the invisible plane that doubles as a time machine. After being rescued from a Perils of Pauline life, Prudence finally realizes her own worth, and also the worth of all women. "From now on," she says proudly to Wonder Woman, "I'll rely on myself, not on a man." Another story ends with Wonder Woman explaining her own long-running romance with Captain Steve Trevor, the American pilot whose crash-landing on Paradise Island was Aphrodite's signal that the strongest and wisest of all the Amazons must answer the call of a war-torn world. As Wonder Woman says of this colleague whom she so often rescues: "I can never love a dominant man."

The most consistent villain is Ares, God of War, a kind of meta-villain who considers women "the natural spoils of war" and insists they stay home as the slaves of men. Otherwise, he fears women will spread their antiwar sentiments, create democracy in the world, and leave him dishonored and unemployed. That's why he keeps trying to trick Queen Hippolyte, Princess Diana's mother, into giving up her powers as Queen of the Amazons, thus allowing him to conquer Paradise Island and destroy the last refuge of ancient feminism. It is in memory of a past time when the Amazons did give in to the soldiers of Ares, and were enslaved by them, that Aphrodite requires each Amazon to wear a pair of cufflike bracelets. If captured and bound by them (as Wonder Woman sometimes is in particularly harrowing episodes), an Amazon loses all her power. Wearing them is a reminder of the fragility of female freedom.

In America, however, villains are marked not only by their violence, but by their prejudice and lust for money. Thomas Tighe, woman-hating industrialist, is typical. After being rescued by Wonder Woman from accidental imprisonment in his own bank vault, he refuses to give her the promised reward of a million dollars. Though the money is needed to support Holliday College, the home of the band of college girls who aid Wonder Woman, Tighe insists that its students must first complete impossible tests of strength and daring. Only after Wonder Woman's powers allow them to meet every challenge does Tighe finally admit: "You win, Wonder Woman! . . . I am no longer a woman hater." She replies: "Then you're the real winner, Mr. Tighe! Because when one ceases to hate, he becomes stronger!"

Other villains are not so easily converted. Chief among them is Dr. Psycho, perhaps a parody of Sigmund Freud. An "evil genius" who "abhors women," the mad doctor's intentions are summed up in this scene-setting preface to an episode called "Battle for Womanhood": "With weird cunning and dark, forbidden knowledge of the occult, Dr. Psycho prepares to change the independent status of modern American women back to the days of the sultans and slave markets, clanking chains and abject captivity. But sly and subtle Psycho reckons without Wonder Woman!"

When I looked into the origins of my proto-feminist super-hero, I discovered that her pseudonymous creator had been a very non-Freudian psychologist named William Moulton Marston. Also a lawyer, businessman, prison reformer, and inventor of the lie-detector test (no doubt the inspiration for Wonder Woman's magic lasso), he had invented Wonder Woman as a heroine for little girls, and also as a conscious alternative to the violence of comic books for boys. In fact, Wonder Woman did attract some boys as readers, but the integrated world of comic book trading revealed her true status: at least three Wonder Woman comic books were necessary to trade for one of Superman. Among the many male super-heroes, only Superman and

Batman were to be as long-lived as Wonder Woman, yet she was still a second-class citizen.

Of course, it's also true that Marston's message wasn't as feminist as it might have been. Instead of portraying the goal of full humanity for women and men, which is what feminism has in mind, he often got stuck in the subject/object, winner/loser paradigm of "masculine" versus "feminine," and came up with female superiority instead. As he wrote: "Women represent love; men represent force. Man's use of force without love brings evil and unhappiness. Wonder Woman proves that women are superior to men because they have love in addition to force." No wonder I was inspired but confused by the isolationism of Paradise Island: Did women have to live separately in order to be happy and courageous? No wonder even boys who could accept equality might have felt less than good about themselves in some of these stories: Were there *any* men who could escape the cultural instruction to be violent?

Wonder Woman herself sometimes got trapped in this either/or choice. As she muses to herself: "Some girls love to have a man stronger than they are to make them do things. Do I like it? I don't know, it's sort of thrilling. But isn't it more fun to make a man obey?" Even female villains weren't capable of being evil on their own. Instead, they were hyperfeminine followers of men's commands. Consider Priscilla Rich, the upper-class antagonist who metamorphoses into the Cheetah, a dangerous she-animal. "Women have been submissive to men," wrote Marston, "and taken men's psychology [force without love] as their own."

In those wartime years, stories could verge on a jingoistic, even racist patriotism. Wonder Woman sometimes forgot her initial shock at America's unjust patriarchal system and confined herself to defeating a sinister foreign threat by proving that women could be just as loyal and brave as men in service of their country. Her costume was a version of the Stars and Stripes. Some of her adversaries were suspiciously short, ugly, fat, or ethnic as a symbol of "un-American" status. In spite of her preaching against violence and for democracy, the good guys were often in uniform, and no country but the United States was seen as a bastion of freedom.

But Marston didn't succumb to stereotypes as often as most comic book writers of the 1940s. Though Prudence, his frontier heroine, is threatened by monosyllabic Indians, Prudence's father turns out to be the true villain, who has been cheating the Indians. And the irrepressible Etta Candy, one of Wonder Woman's band of college girls, is surely one of the few fat-girl heroines in comics.

There are other unusual rewards. Queen Hippolyte, for instance, is a rare example of a mother who is good, powerful, and a mentor to her daughter. She founds nations, fights to protect Paradise Island, and is a source of strength to Wonder Woman as she battles the forces of evil and inequality. Mother and daughter stay in touch through a sort of telepathic TV set, and the result is a team of equals who are separated only by experience. In the flashback episode in which Queen Hippolyte succumbs to Hercules, she is even seen as a sexual being. How many girl children grew to adulthood with no such example of a strong, sensual mother—except for these slender stories? How many mothers preferred sons, or believed the patriarchal myth that competition is "natural" between mothers and daughters, or tamed their daughters instead of encouraging their wildness and strength? We are just beginning to realize the sense of anger and loss in girls whose mothers had no power to protect them, or forced them to conform out of fear for their safety, or left them to identify only with their fathers if they had any ambition at all.

Finally, there is Wonder Woman's ability to unleash the power of self-respect within the women around her; to help them work together and support each other. This may not seem revolutionary to male readers accustomed to stories that depict men working together, but for females who are usually seen as competing for the favors of men—especially little girls who may just be getting to the age when girlfriends betray each other for the approval of boys—this discovery of sisterhood can be exhilarating indeed. Women get a rare message of independence, of depending on themselves, not even on Wonder Woman. "You saved yourselves," as she says in one of her inevitable morals at story's end. "I only showed you that you could."

Whatever the shortcomings of William Marston, his virtues became clear after his death in 1947. Looking back at the post-Marston stories I had missed the first time around—for at twelve or thirteen, I thought I had outgrown Wonder Woman and had abandoned her—I could see how little her later writers understood her spirit. She became sexier-looking and more submissive, violent episodes increased, more of her adversaries were female, and Wonder Woman herself required more help from men in order to triumph. Like so many of her real-life sisters in the postwar era of conservatism and "togetherness" of the 1950s, she had fallen on very hard times.

By the 1960s, Wonder Woman had given up her magic lasso, her bullet-deflecting bracelets, her invisible plane, and all her Amazonian powers. Though she still had adventures and even practiced karate, any attractive man could disarm her. She had become a kind of female James Bond, though much more boring because she was denied his sexual freedom. She was Diana Prince, a mortal who walked about in boutique, car-hop clothes and took the advice of a male mastermind named "I Ching."

It was in this sad state that I first rediscovered my Amazon super-hero in 1972. *Ms.* magazine had just begun, and we were looking for a cover story for its first regular issue to appear in July. Since Joanne Edgar and other of its founding editors had also been rescued by Wonder Woman in their childhoods, we decided to rescue Wonder Woman in return. Though it wasn't easy to persuade her publishers to let us put her original image on the cover of a new and unknown feminist magazine, or to reprint her 1940s Golden Age episodes inside, we finally succeeded. Wonder Woman appeared on news-stands again in all her original glory, striding through city streets like a colossus, stopping planes and bombs with one hand and rescuing buildings with the other.

Clearly, there were many nostalgic grown-ups and heroine-starved readers of all ages. The consensus of response seemed to be that if we had all read more about Wonder Woman and less about Dick and Jane, we might have been a lot better off. As for her publishers, they, too, were impressed. Under the direction of Dorothy Woolfolk, the first woman editor of Wonder Woman in all her long history, she was re-turned to her original Amazon status—golden lasso, bracelets, and all.

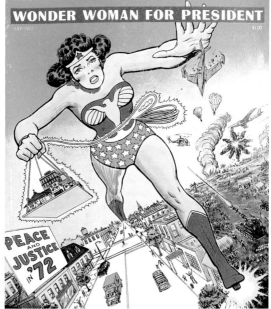

16

One day some months after her rebirth, I got a phone call from one of Wonder Woman's tougher male writers. "Okay," he said, "she's got all her Amazon powers back. She talks to the Amazons on Paradise Island. She even has a Black Amazon sister named Nubia. Now will you leave me alone?"

I said we would.

In the 1970s, Wonder Woman became the star of a television series. As played by Lynda Carter, she was a little blue of eye and large of breast, but she still retained her Amazon powers, her ability to convert instead of kill, and her appeal for many young female viewers. There were some who refused to leave their TV sets on Wonder Woman night. A few young boys even began to dress up as Wonder Woman on Halloween—a true revolution.

In the 1980s, Wonder Woman's story line was revamped by DC Comics, which reinvented its male super-heroes Superman and Batman at about the same time. Steve Trevor became a veteran of Vietnam; he remained a friend, but was romantically involved with Etta Candy. Wonder Woman acquired a Katharine Hepburn–Spencer Tracy relationship with a street-smart Boston detective named Ed Indelicato, whose tough-guy attitude played off Wonder Woman's idealism. She also gained a friend and surrogate mother in Julia Kapatelis, a leading archaeologist and professor of Greek culture at Harvard University who can understand the ancient Greek that is Wonder Woman's native tongue, and be a model of a smart, caring, single mother for girl readers. Julia's teenage daughter, Vanessa, is the age of many readers and goes through all of their uncertainties, trials, and tribulations, but has the joy of having a powerful older sister in Wonder Woman. There is even Myndi Mayer, a slick Hollywood public relations agent who turns Wonder Woman into America's hero, and is also in constant danger of betraying Diana's idealistic spirit. In other words, there are many of the currents of society today, from single mothers to the worries of teenage daughters and a commercial culture, instead of the simpler plots of America's dangers in World War II.

You will see whether Wonder Woman carries her true Amazon spirit into the present. If not, let her publishers know. She belongs to you.

Since Wonder Woman's beginnings more than a half century ago, however, a strange thing has happened: the Amazon myth has been rethought as archaeological relics have come to light. Though Amazons had been considered figments of the imagination, perhaps the mythological evidence of man's fear of woman, there is a tentative but growing body of evidence to support the theory that some Amazon-like societies did exist. In Europe, graves once thought to contain male skeletons—because they were buried with weapons or were killed by battle wounds—have turned out to hold skeletons of females after all. In the jungles of Brazil, scientists have found caves of what appears to have been an all-female society. The caves are strikingly devoid of the usual phallic design and theme; they feature, instead, the triangular female symbol, and the only cave that does bear male designs is believed to have been the copulatorium, where Amazons mated with males from surrounding tribes, kept only the female children, and returned male infants to the tribe. Such archaeological finds have turned up not only along the Amazon River in Brazil, but at the foot of the Atlas Mountains in northwestern Africa, and on the European and Asiatic sides of the Black Sea.

There is still far more controversy than agreement, but a shared supposition of these myths is this: imposing patriarchy on the gynocracy of prehistory took many centuries and great cruelty. Rather than give up freedom and worship only male gods, some bands of women resisted. They formed all-woman cultures that survived by capturing men from local tribes, mating with them, and raising their girl children to have great skills of body and mind. These bands became warriors and healers who were sometimes employed for their skills by patriarchal cultures around them. As a backlash culture, they were doomed, but they may also have lasted for centuries.

Perhaps that's the appeal of Wonder Woman, Paradise Island, and this comic book message. It's not only a child's need for a lost independence, but an adult's need for a lost balance between women and men, between humans and nature. As the new Wonder Woman says to Vanessa, "Remember your *power*, little sister."

However simplified, that is Wonder Woman's message: Remember Our Power.

LIST OF ARTISTS

Numerals refer to page numbers, not issue numbers.

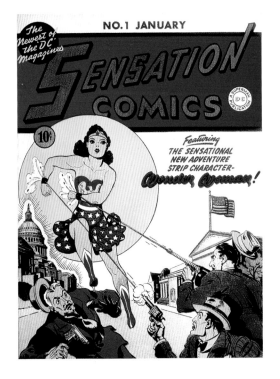

JANUARY 1942; NO. 1
Cover artist: Harry G. Peter

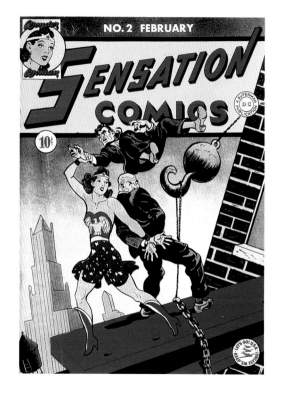

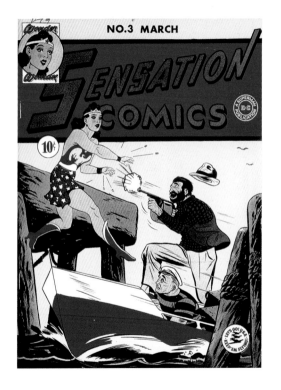

MARCH 1942; NO. 3
Cover artist: Harry G. Peter

APRIL 1942; NO. 4
Cover artist: Harry G. Peter

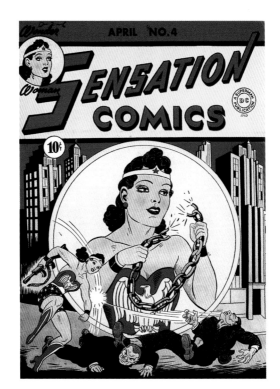

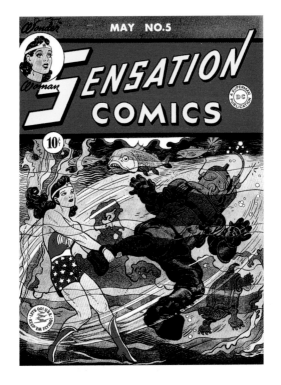

MAY 1942; NO. 5
Cover artist: Harry G. Peter

SUMMER 1942; NO. 1
Cover artist: Harry G. Peter

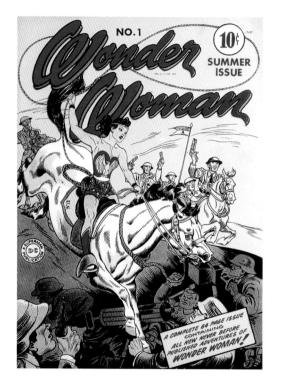

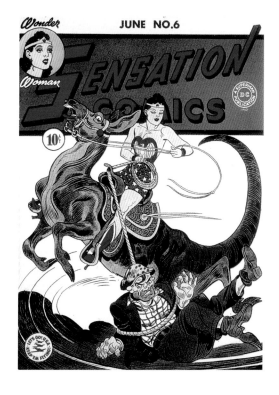

JUNE 1942; NO. 6
Cover artist: Harry G. Peter

JUNE-JULY 1942; NO. 11
Cover artist: Sheldon Moldoff

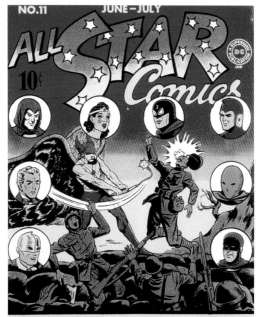

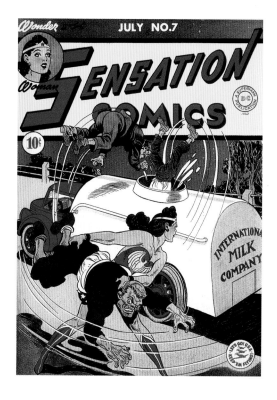

JULY 1942; NO. 7
Cover artist: Harry G. Peter

AUGUST 1942; NO. 8
Cover artist: Harry G. Peter

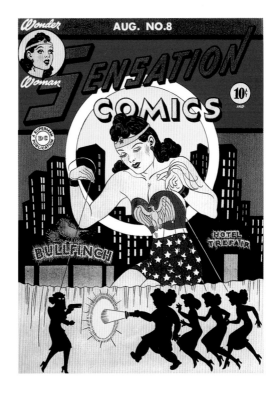

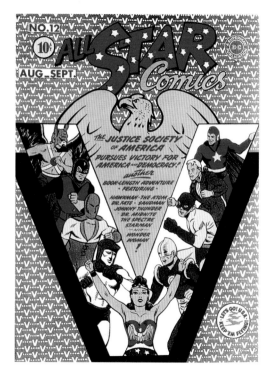

AUGUST–SEPTEMBER 1942; NO. 12

Cover artist: Jack Burnley

FALL 1942; NO. 2
Cover artist: Harry G. Peter

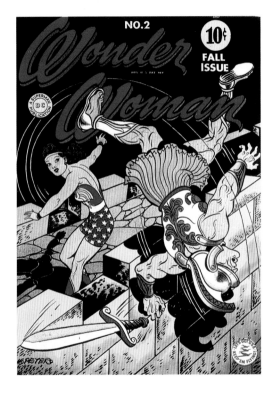

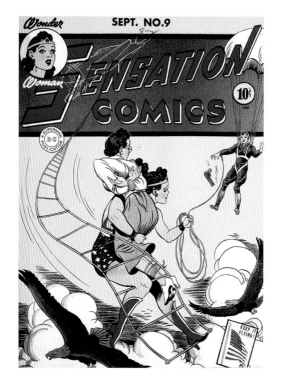

SEPTEMBER 1942; NO. 9
Cover artist: Harry G. Peter

OCTOBER 1942; NO. 10
Cover artist: Harry G. Peter

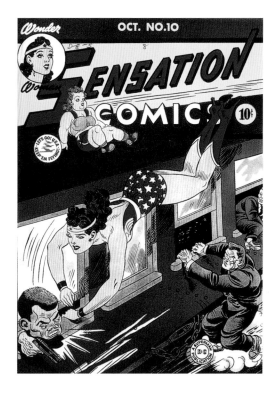

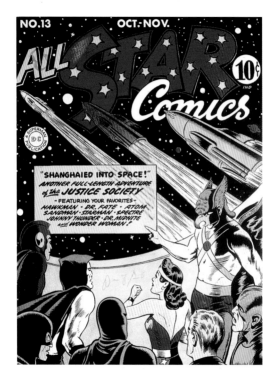

OCTOBER–NOVEMBER 1942; NO. 13

Cover artist: Jack Burnley

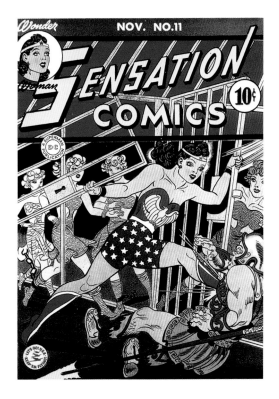

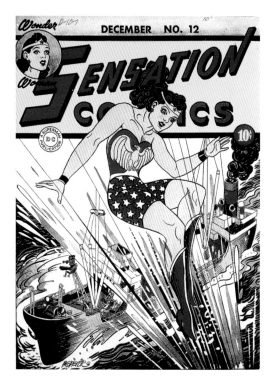

DECEMBER 1942; NO. 12

Cover artist: Harry G. Peter

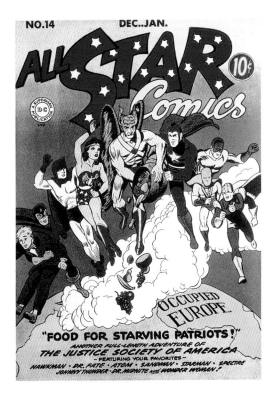

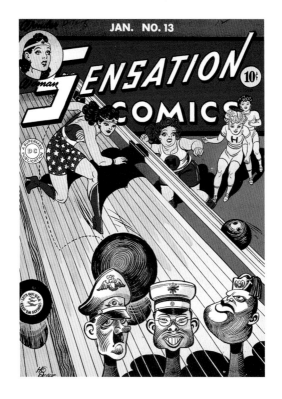

JANUARY 1943; NO. 13

Cover artist: Harry G. Peter

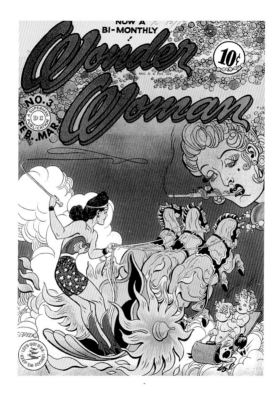

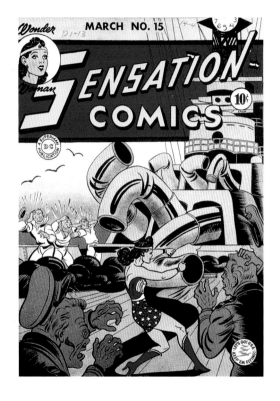

MARCH 1943: NO. 15

Cover artist: Harry G. Peter

APRIL–MAY 1943; NO. 16
Cover artist: Frank Harry

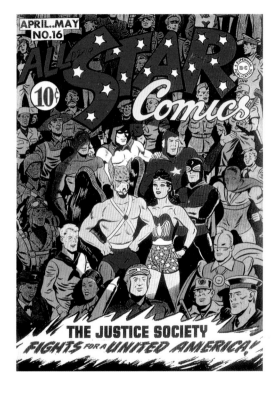

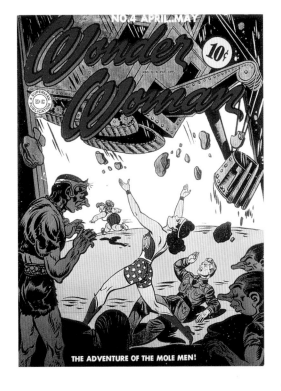

APRIL–MAY 1943; NO. 4

Cover artist: Harry G. Peter

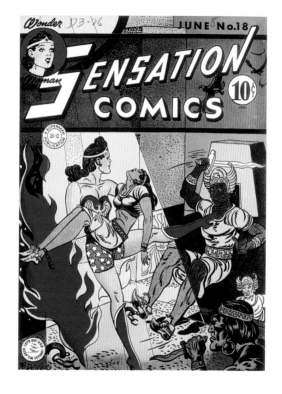

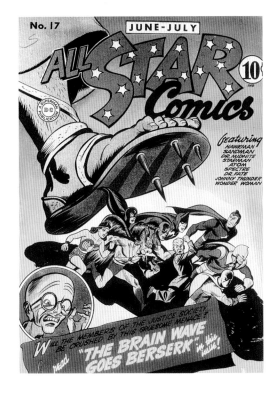

JUNE-JULY 1943; NO. 17

Cover artist: Joe Gallagher

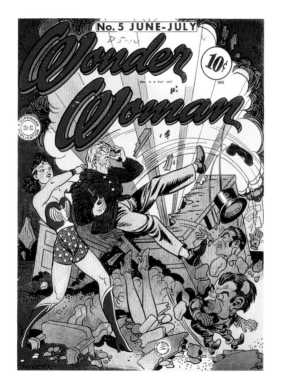

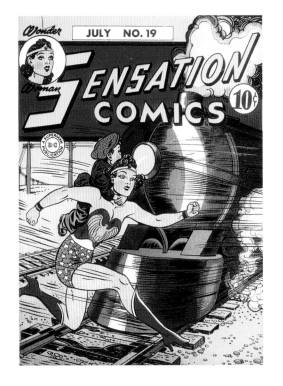

JULY 1943; NO. 19
Cover artist: Harry G. Peter

FALL 1943; NO. 6
Cover artist: Harry G. Peter

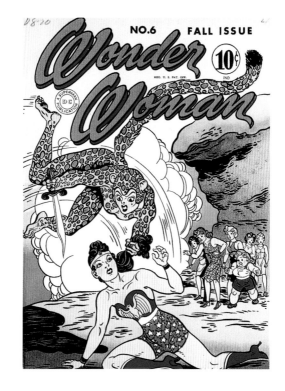

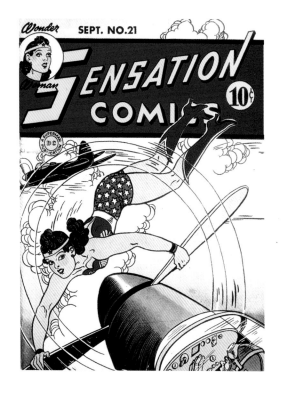

SEPTEMBER 1943; NO. 21
Cover artist: Harry G. Peter

WINTER 1943–44; NO. 19
Cover artist: Joe Gallagher

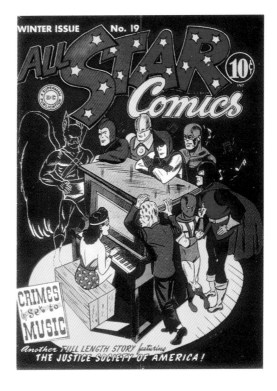

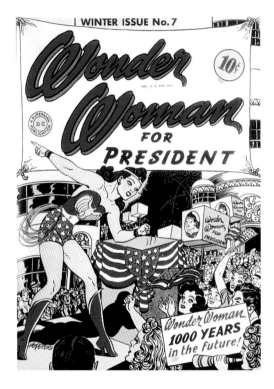

WINTER 1943; NO. 7

Cover artist: Harry G. Peter

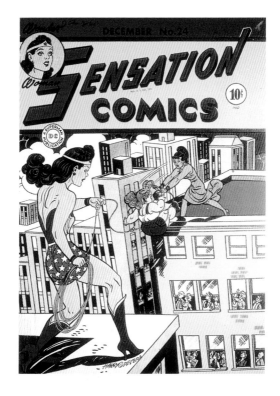

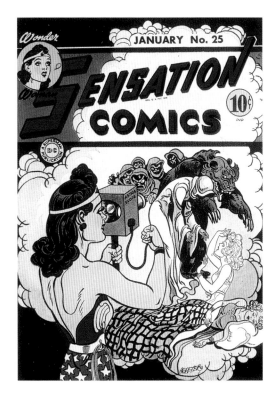

JANUARY 1944; NO. 25

Cover artist: Harry G. Peter

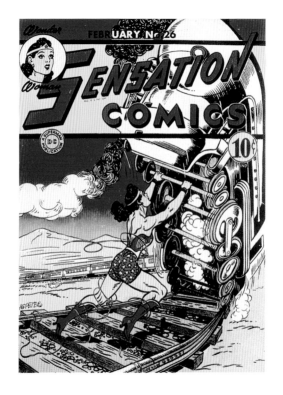

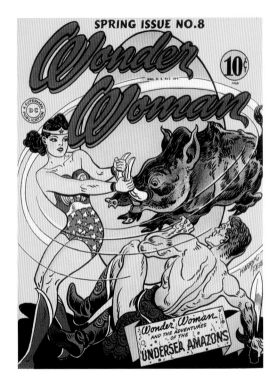

SPRING 1944; NO. 8
Cover artist: Harry G. Peter

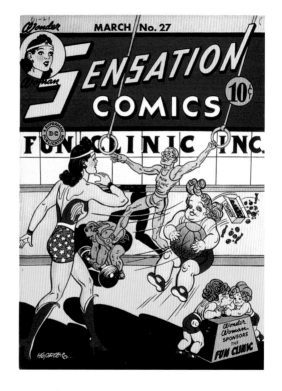

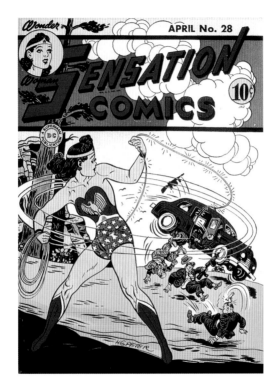

APRIL 1944; NO. 28

Cover artist: Harry G. Peter

SUMMER 1944; NO. 9
Cover artist: Harry G. Peter

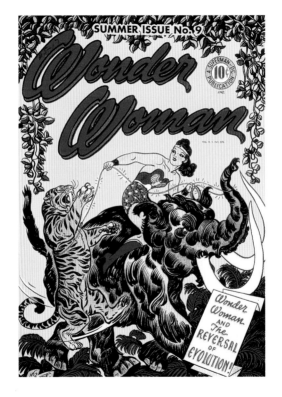

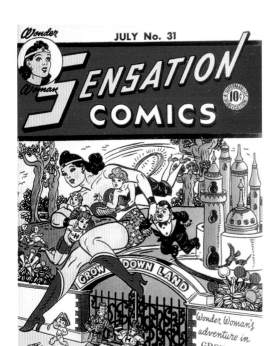

JULY 1944; NO. 31
Cover artist: Harry G. Peter

AUGUST 1944; NO. 32
Cover artist: Harry G. Peter

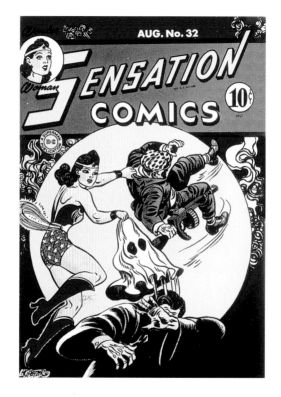

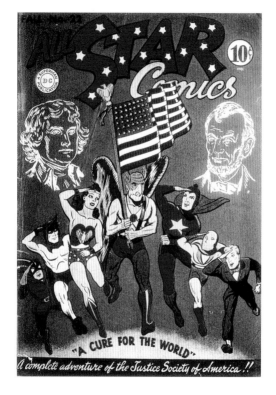

FALL 1944; NO. 22
Cover artist: Frank Harry

FALL 1944; NO. 10
Cover artist: Harry G. Peter

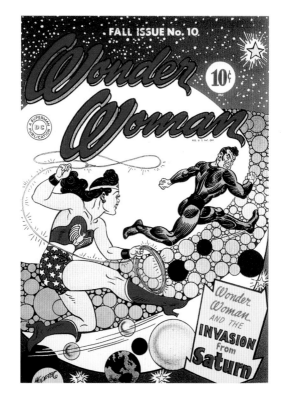

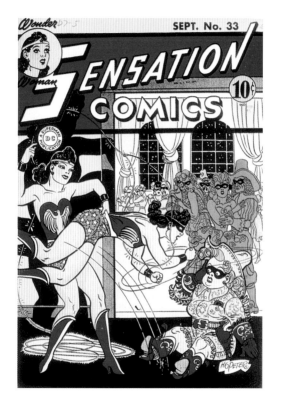

SEPTEMBER 1944; NO. 33

Cover artist: Harry G. Peter

NOVEMBER 1944; NO. 35
Cover artist: Harry G. Peter

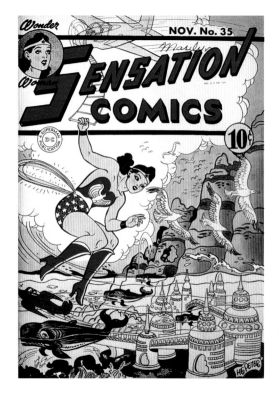

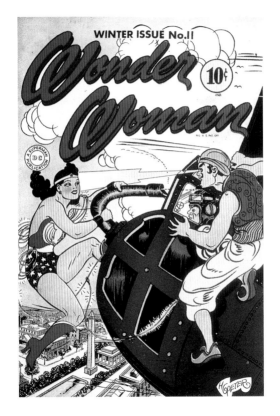

WINTER 1944; NO. 11

Cover artist: Harry G. Peter

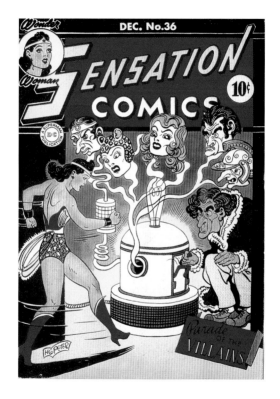

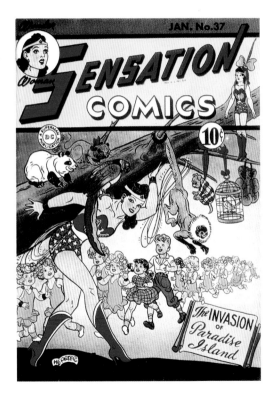

JANUARY 1945; NO. 37

Cover artist: Harry G. Peter

FEBRUARY 1945; NO. 38
Cover artist: Harry G. Peter

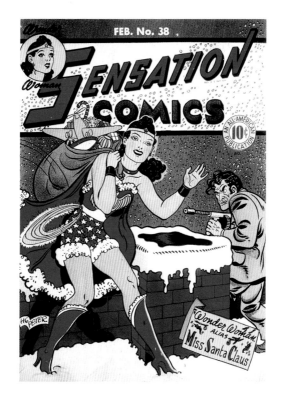

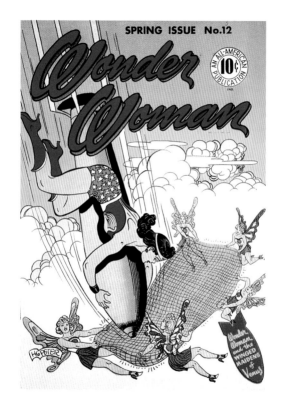

SPRING 1945; NO. 12

Cover artist: Harry G. Peter

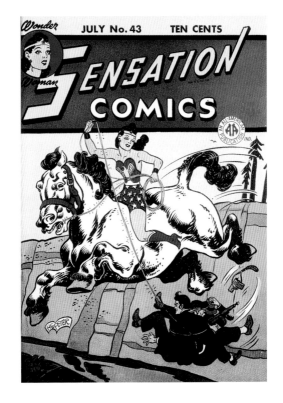

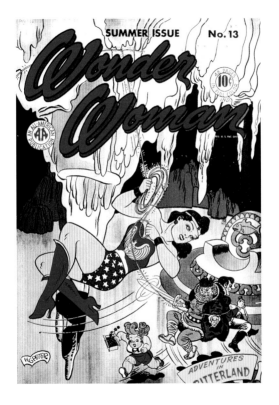

SUMMER 1945; NO. 13

Cover artist: Harry G. Peter

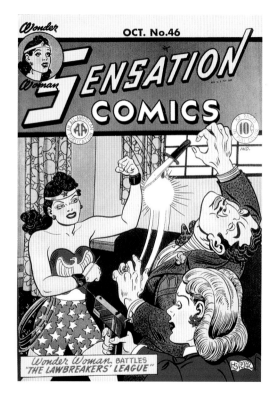

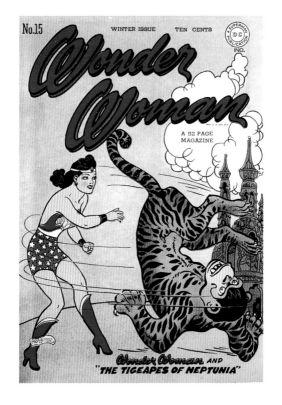

WINTER 1945; NO. 15
Cover artist: Harry G. Peter

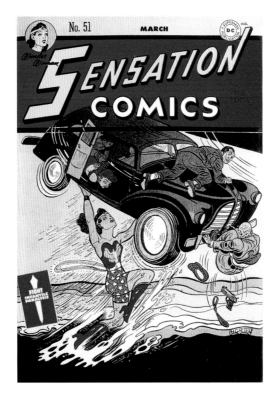

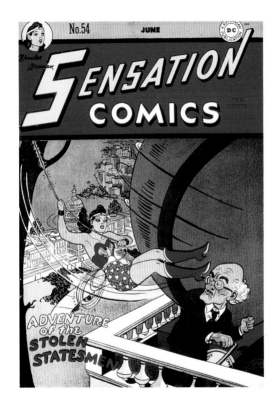

JUNE 1946; NO. 54
Cover artist: Harry G. Peter

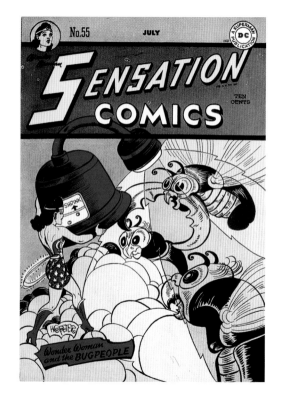

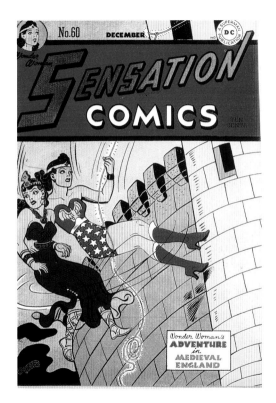

DECEMBER 1946; NO. 60

Cover artist: Harry G. Peter

JANUARY–FEBRUARY 1947; NO. 21
Cover artist: Harry G. Peter

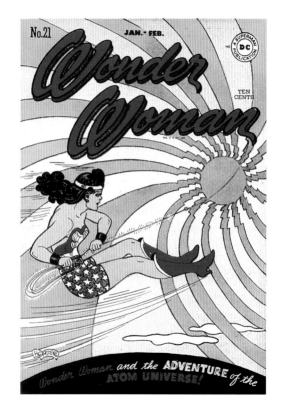

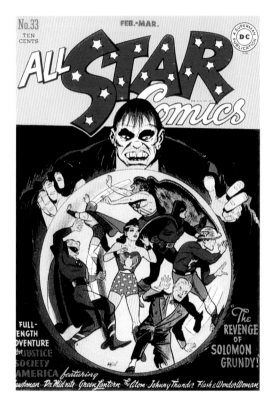

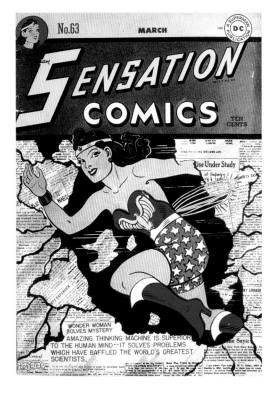

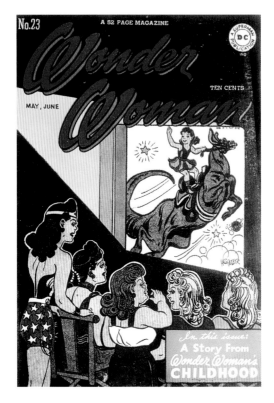

MAY-JUNE 1947; NO. 23
Cover artist: Harry G. Peter

JUNE 1947; NO. 66
Cover artist: Harry G. Peter

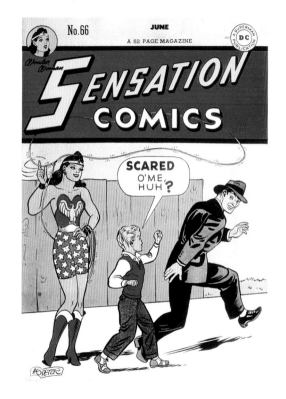

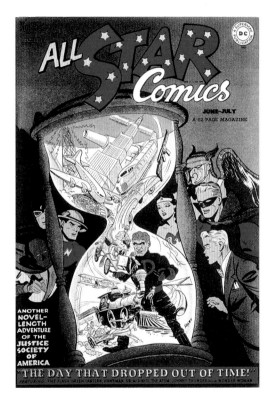

JUNE-JULY 1947; NO. 35

Cover artist: Irwin Hasen

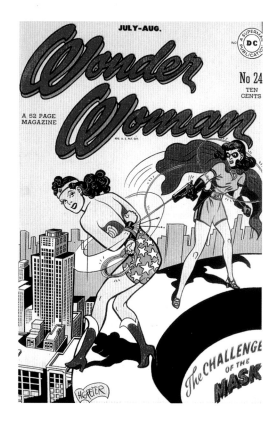

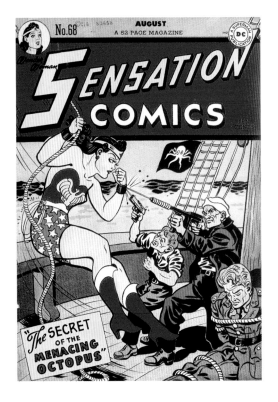

AUGUST 1947; NO. 68

Cover artist: Harry G. Peter

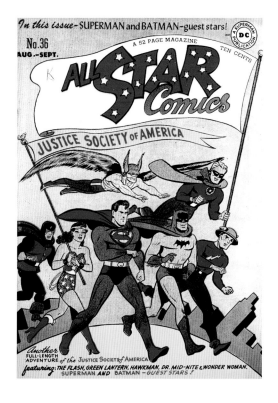

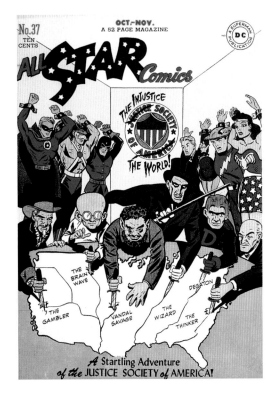

OCTOBER–NOVEMBER 1947; NO. 37

Cover artist: Irwin Hasen

NOVEMBER 1947; NO. 71
Cover artist: Harry G. Peter

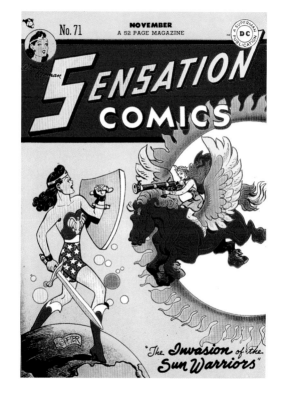

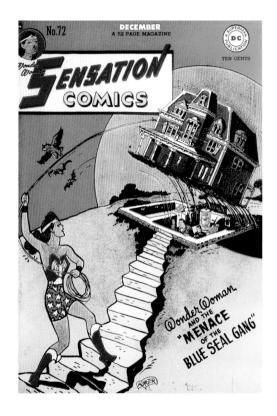

DECEMBER 1947; NO. 72
Cover artist: Harry G. Peter

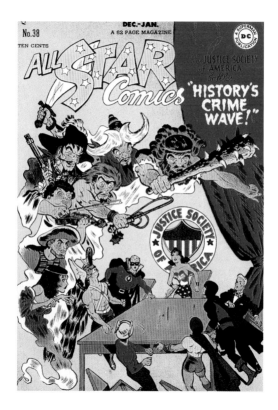

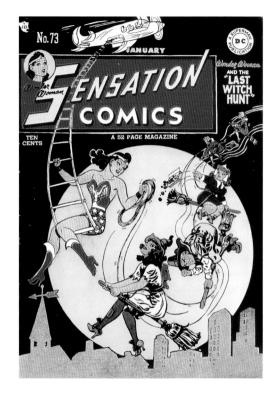

JANUARY 1948; NO. 73

Cover artist: Harry G. Peter

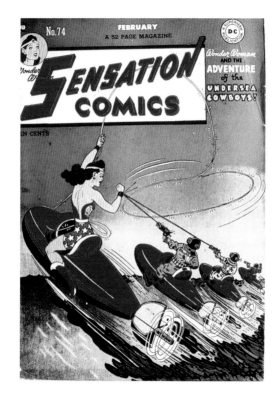

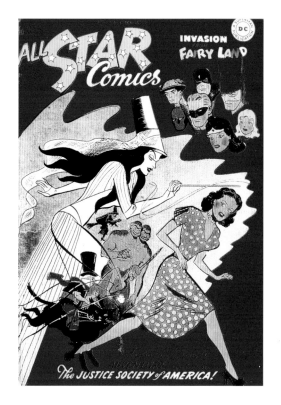

FEBRUARY–MARCH 1948; NO. 39
Cover artist: Irwin Hasen

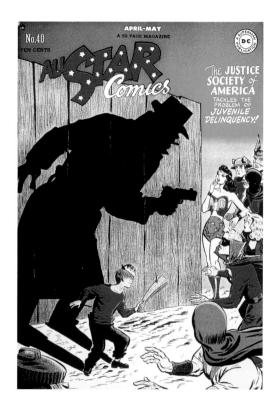

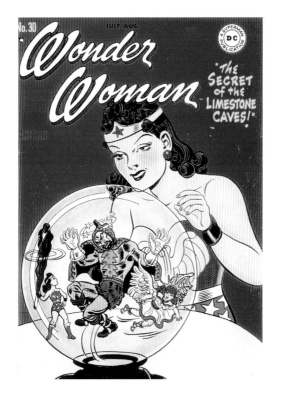

JULY-AUGUST 1948; NO. 30

Cover artist: Harry G. Peter

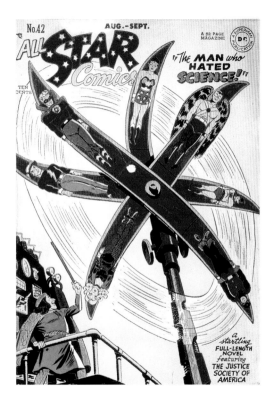

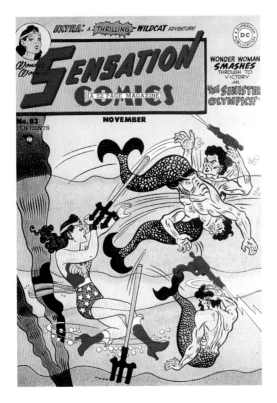

NOVEMBER 1948; NO. 83
Cover artist: Harry G. Peter

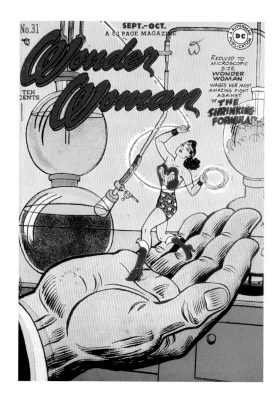

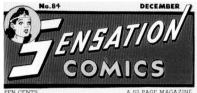

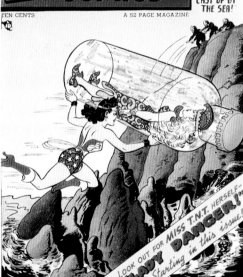

DECEMBER 1948; NO. 84
Cover artist: Harry G. Peter

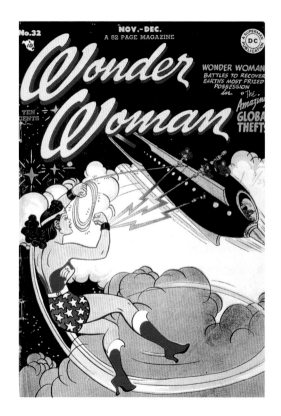

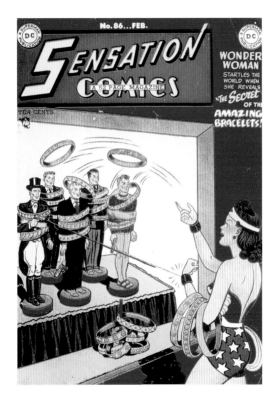

FEBRUARY 1949; NO. 86

Cover artist: Harry G. Peter

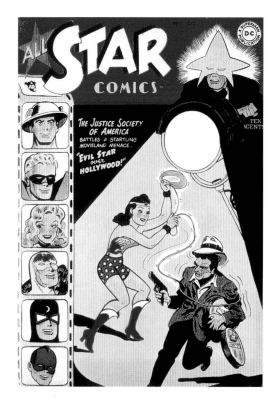

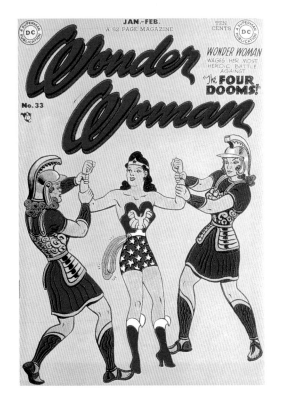

FEBRUARY–MARCH 1949; NO. 45
Cover artists: Irwin Hasen, Bob Oksner

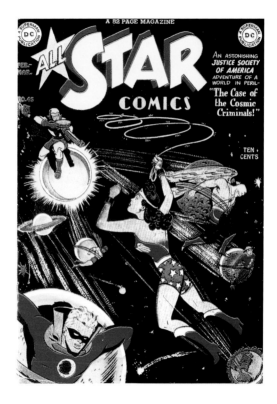

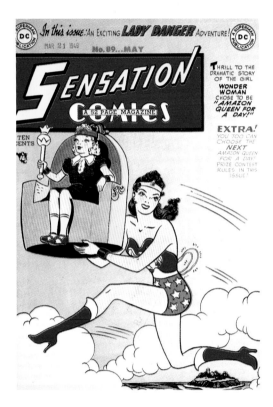

MAY 1949; NO. 89

Cover artist: Harry G. Peter

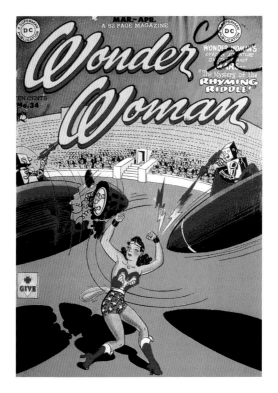

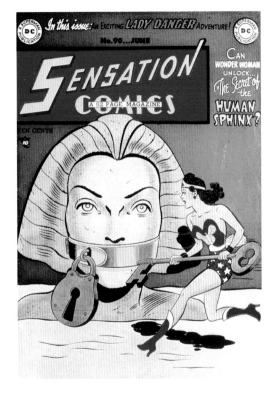

APRIL–MAY 1949; NO. 46
Cover artists: Arthur Peddy, Bernard Sachs

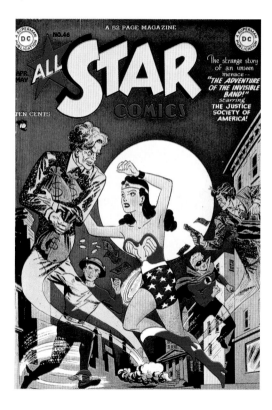

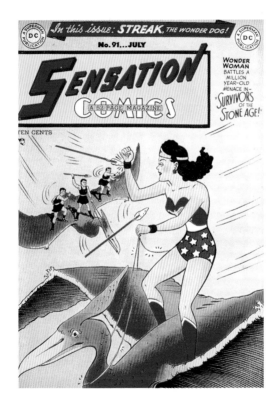

JULY 1949; NO. 91
Cover artist: Harry G. Peter

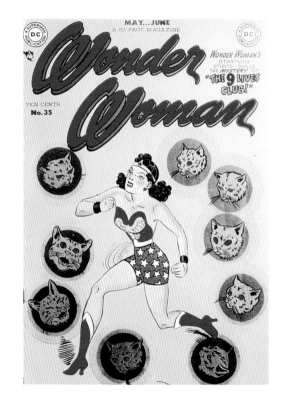

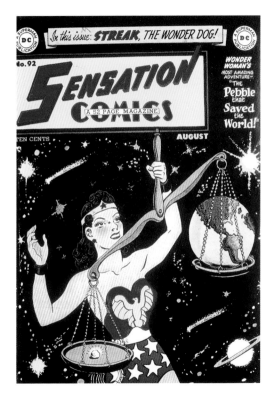

AUGUST 1949; NO. 92

Cover artist: Harry G. Peter

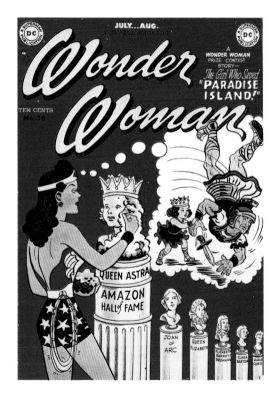

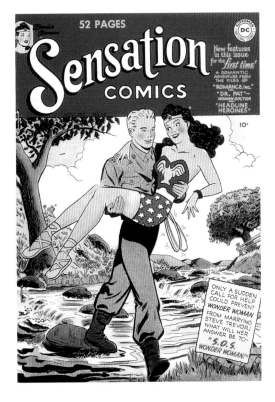

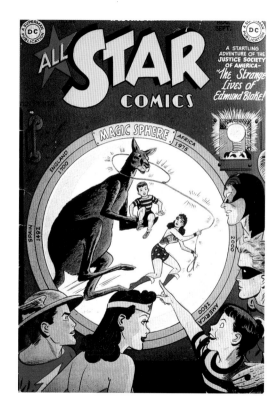

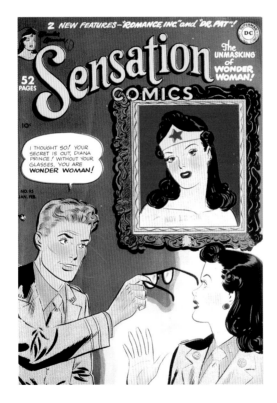

SEPTEMBER–OCTOBER 1949; NO. 37
Cover artist: Harry G. Peter

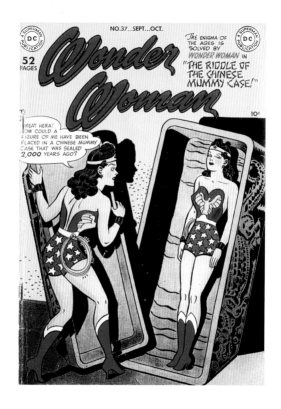

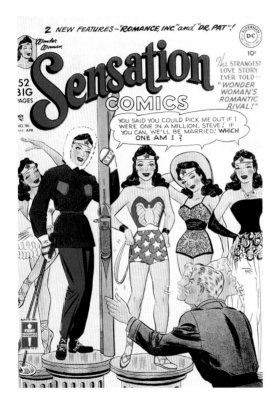

MARCH–APRIL 1950; NO. 96

Cover artists: Irwin Hasen, Bernard Sachs

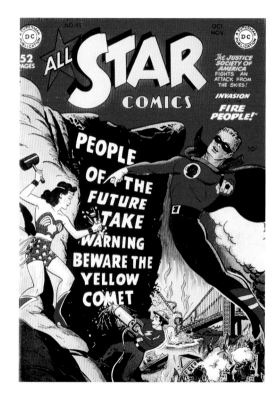

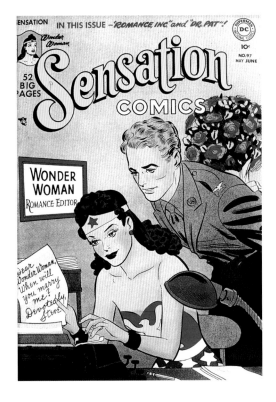

MAY-JUNE 1950; NO. 97
Cover artist: Irwin Hasen

NOVEMBER–DECEMBER 1949; NO. 38
Cover artist: Harry G. Peter

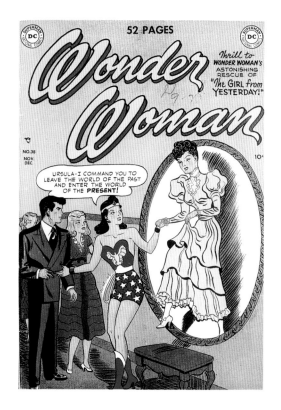

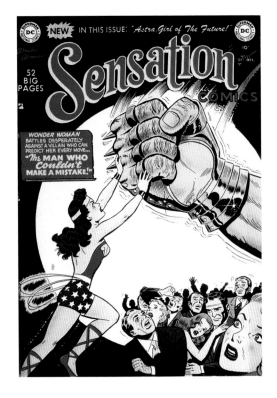

SEPTEMBER–OCTOBER 1950; NO. 99
Cover artists: Irwin Hasen, Bernard Sachs

NOVEMBER–DECEMBER 1950; NO. 100
Cover artists: Irwin Hasen, Bernard Sachs

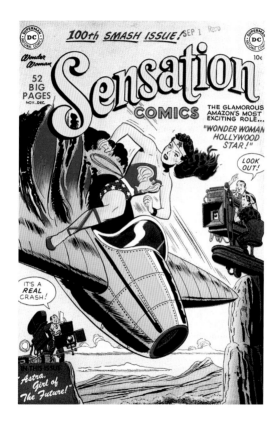

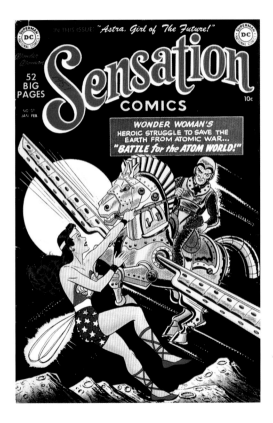

JANUARY-FEBRUARY 1951; NO. 101
Cover artists: Irwin Hasen, Bernard Sachs

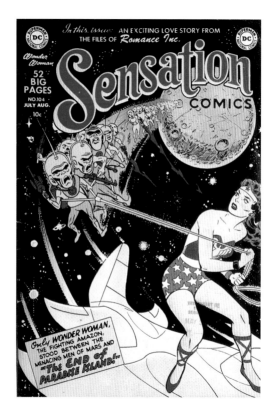

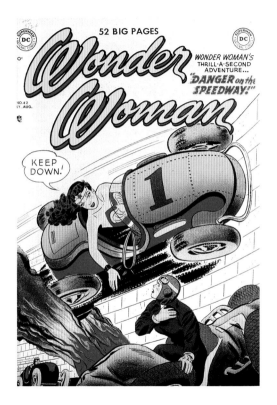

JULY-AUGUST 1950; NO. 42
Cover artists: Irwin Hasen, Bernard Sachs

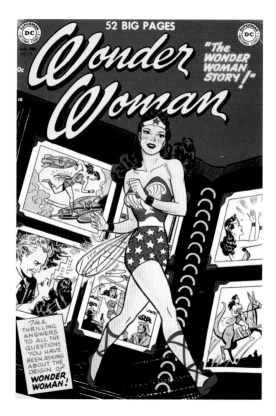

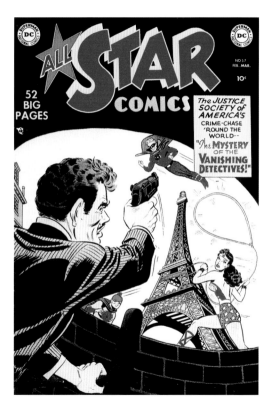

FEBRUARY–MARCH 1951; NO. 57

Cover artists: Arthur Peddy, Bernard Sachs

MARCH–APRIL 1951; NO. 46
Cover artists: Irwin Hasen, Bernard Sachs

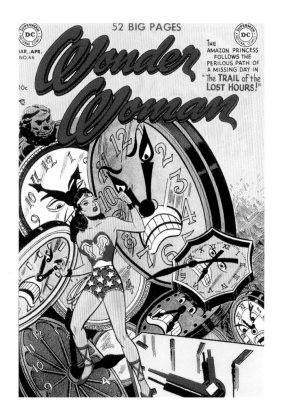

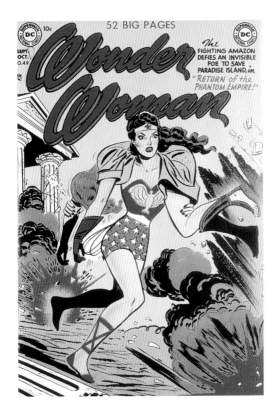

SEPTEMBER–OCTOBER 1951; NO. 49
Cover artists: Irwin Hasen, Bernard Sachs

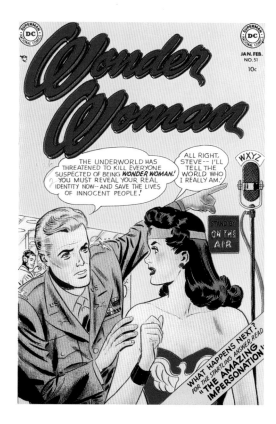

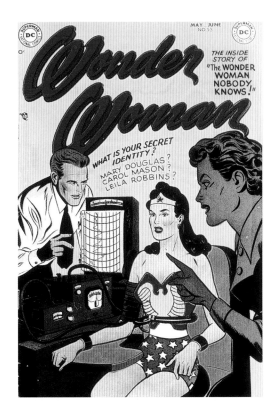

MAY–JUNE 1952; NO. 53
Cover artist: Irwin Hasen

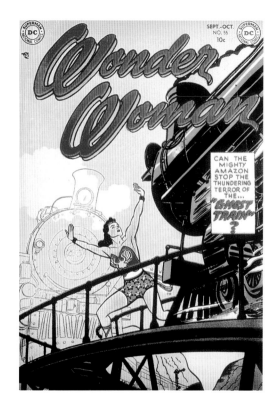

JANUARY-FEBRUARY 1953 NO. 57
Cover artists: Irwin Hasen, Bernard Sachs

MARCH–APRIL 1953 NO. 58
Cover artists: Irwin Hasen, Bernard Sachs

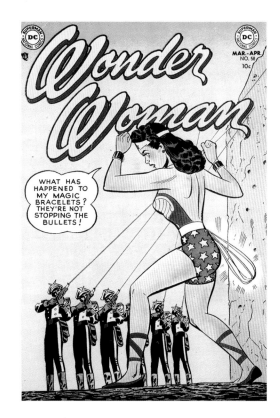

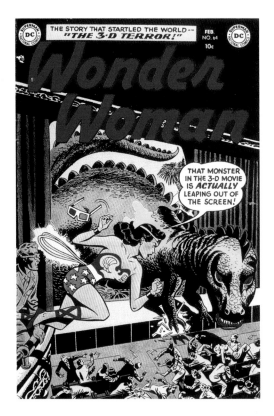

FEBRUARY 1954; NO. 64

Cover artists: Irwin Hasen, Bernard Sachs

JULY 1955; NO. 75
Cover artists: Irwin Hasen, Bernard Sachs

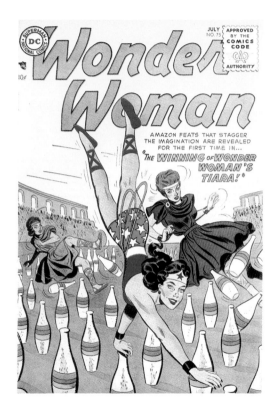

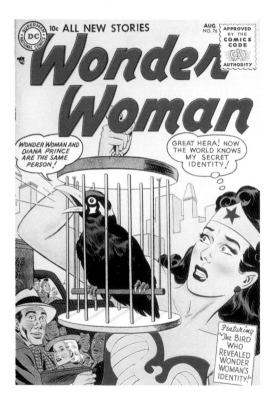

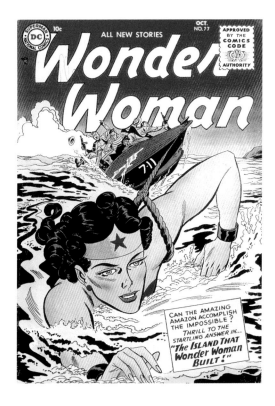

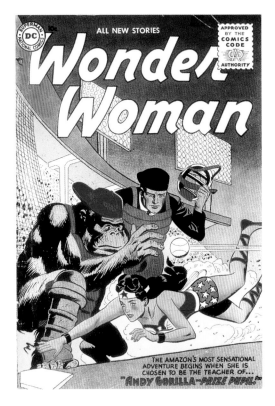

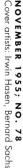

NOVEMBER 1955; NO. 78

Cover artists: Irwin Hasen, Bernard Sachs

JANUARY 1956; NO. 79
Cover artists: Irwin Hasen, Bernard Sachs

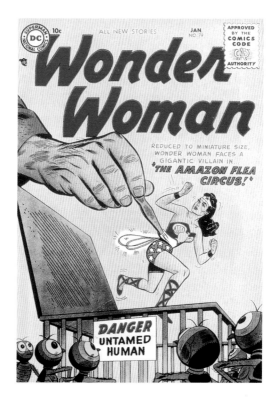

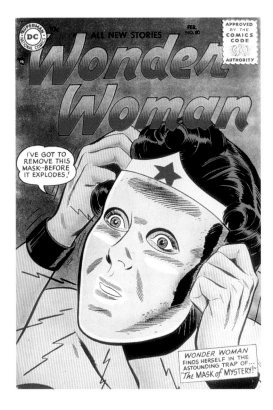

FEBRUARY 1956; NO. 80

Cover artists: Irwin Hasen, Bernard Sachs

141

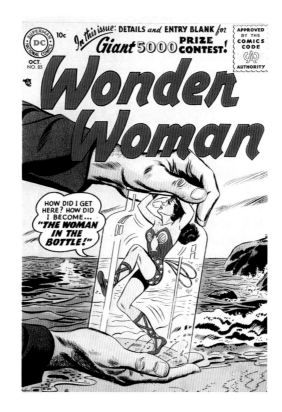

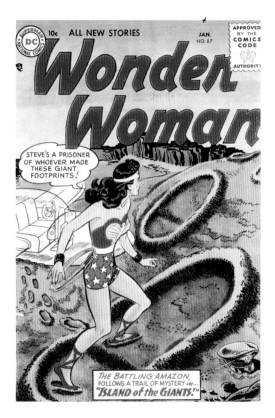

JANUARY 1957; NO. 87
Cover artist: Irv Novick

143

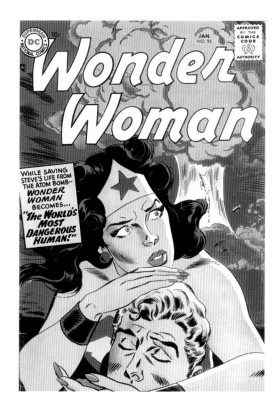

JANUARY 1958; NO. 95
Cover artists: Ross Andru, Mike Esposito

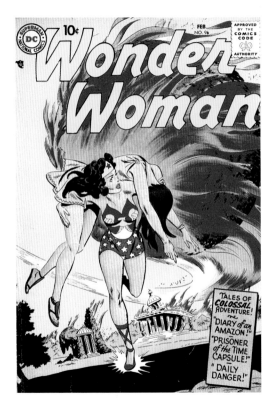

FEBRUARY 1958; NO. 96
Cover artists: Ross Andru, Mike Esposito

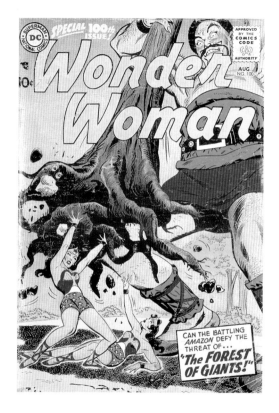

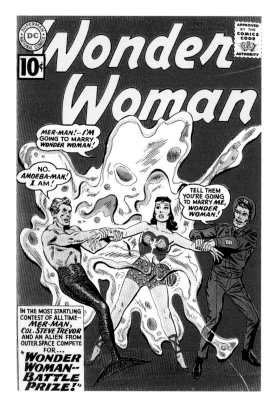

OCTOBER 1961; NO. 125
Cover artists: Ross Andru, Mike Esposito

147

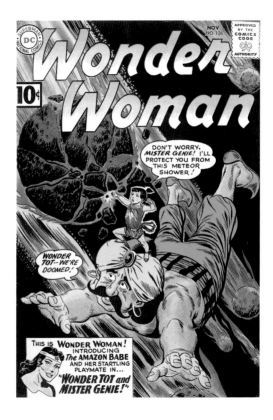

NOVEMBER 1961; NO. 126
Cover artists: Ross Andru, Mike Esposito

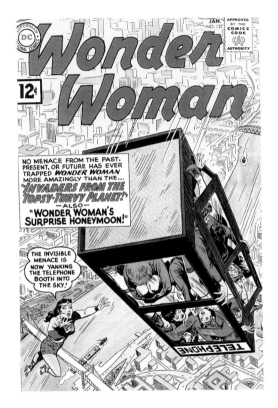

JANUARY 1962; NO. 127
Cover artists: Ross Andru, Mike Esposito

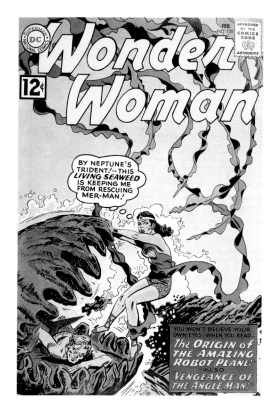

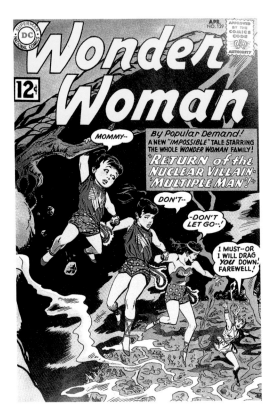

APRIL 1962; NO. 129
Cover artists: Ross Andru, Mike Esposito

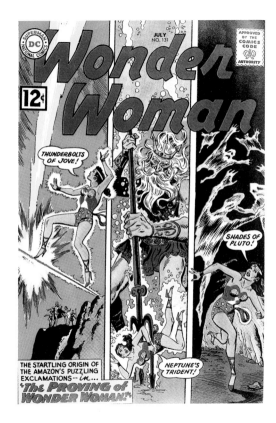

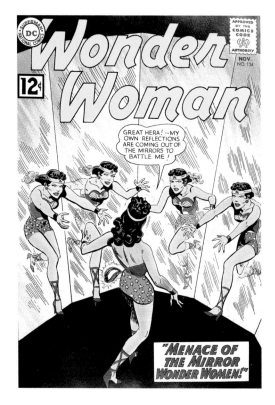

NOVEMBER 1962; NO. 134

Cover artists: Ross Andru, Mike Esposito

JANUARY 1963; NO. 135
Cover artists: Ross Andru, Mike Esposito

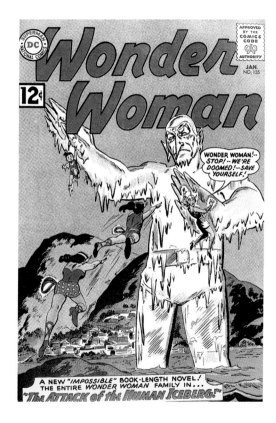

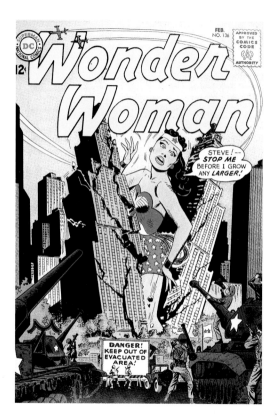

FEBRUARY 1963; NO. 136
Cover artists: Ross Andru, Mike Esposito

APRIL 1963: NO. 137
Cover artists: Ross Andru, Mike Esposito

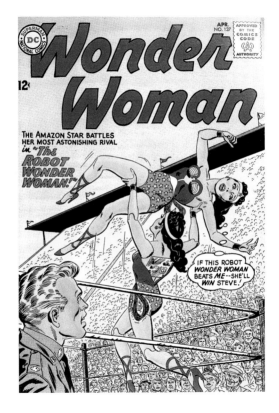

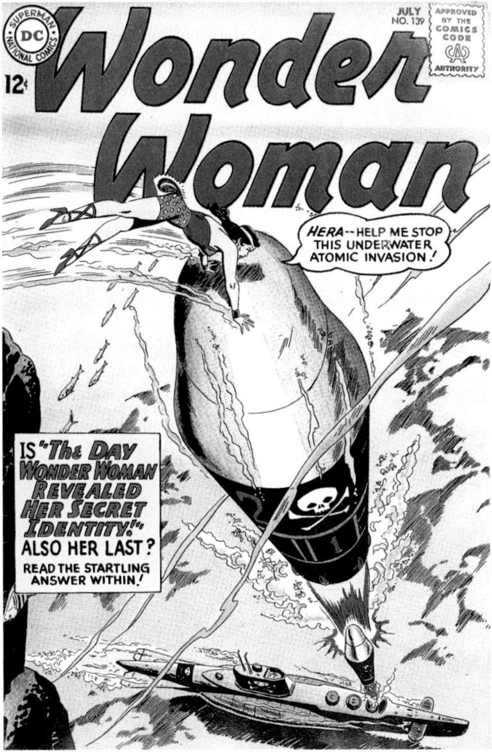

JULY 1963; NO. 139
Cover artists: Ross Andru, Mike Esposito

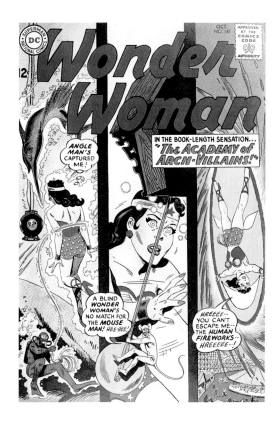

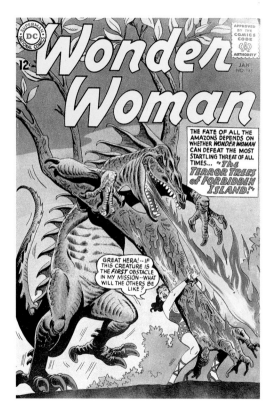

JANUARY 1964: NO. 143
Cover artists: Ross Andru, Mike Esposito

FEBRUARY 1964; NO. 144
Cover artists: Ross Andru, Mike Esposito

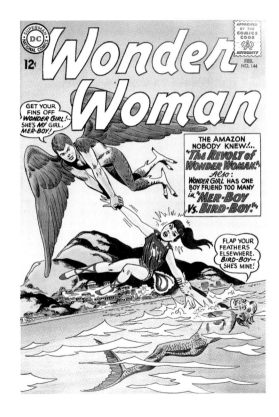

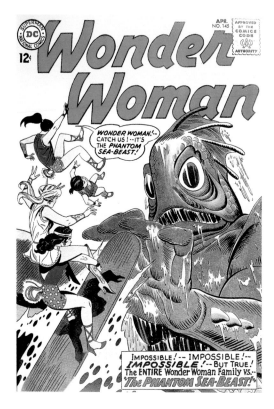

APRIL 1964; NO. 145
Cover artists: Ross Andru, Mike Esposito

AUGUST 1964; NO. 148
Cover artists: Ross Andru, Mike Esposito

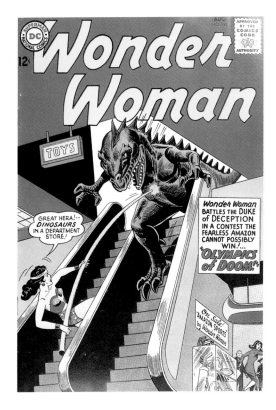

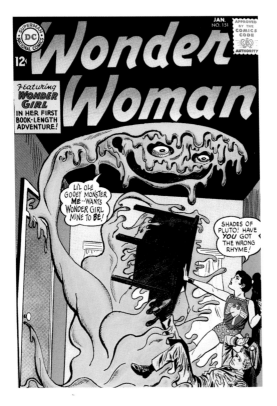

JANUARY 1965; NO. 151
Cover artists: Ross Andru, Mike Esposito

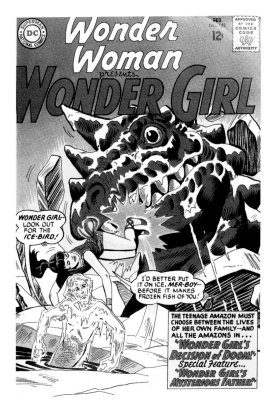

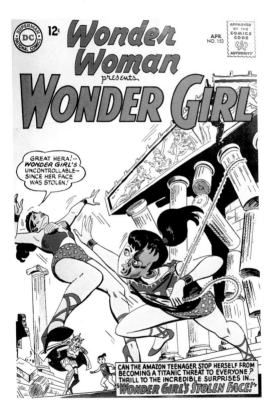

APRIL 1965; NO. 153
Cover artists: Ross Andru, Mike Esposito

MAY 1965; NO. 154

Cover artists: Ross Andru, Mike Esposito

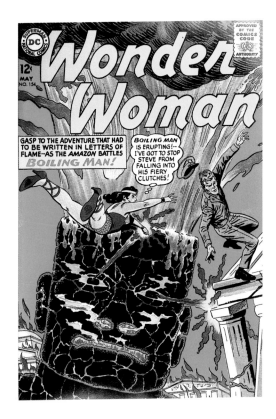

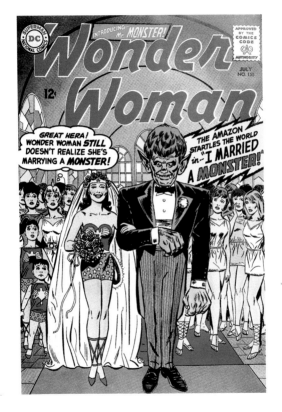

JULY 1965; NO. 155
Cover artists: Ross Andru, Mike Esposito

AUGUST 1965; NO. 156
Cover artists: Ross Andru, Mike Esposito

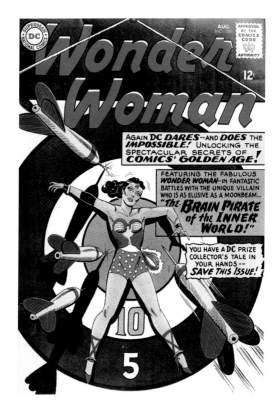

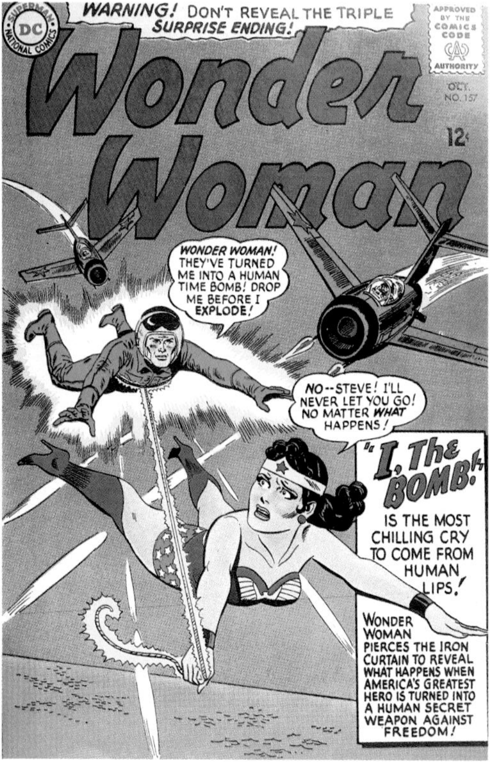

OCTOBER 1965; NO. 157
Cover artists: Ross Andru, Mike Esposito

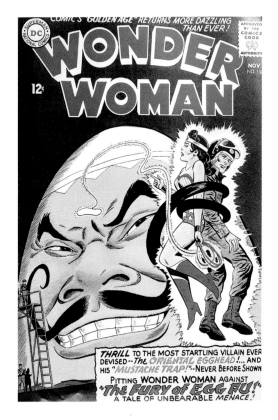

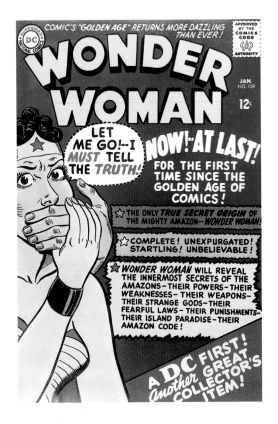

JANUARY 1966; NO. 159
Cover artists: Ross Andru, Mike Esposito

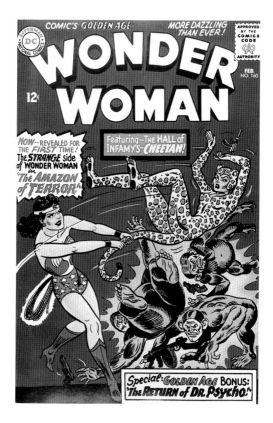

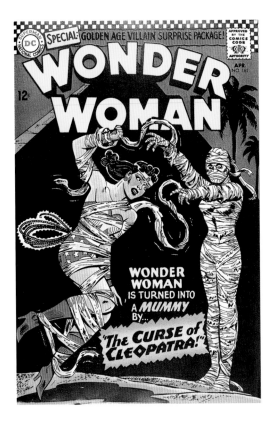

APRIL 1966; NO. 161

Cover artists: Ross Andru, Mike Esposito

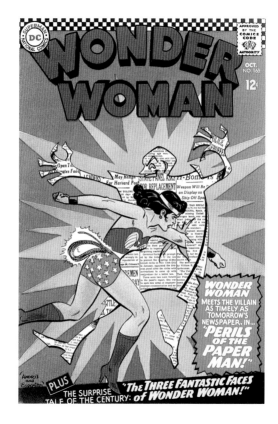

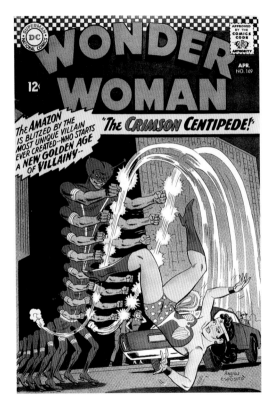

APRIL 1967; NO. 169
Cover artists: Ross Andru, Mike Esposito

MAY–JUNE 1968; NO. 176
Cover artist: Irv Novick

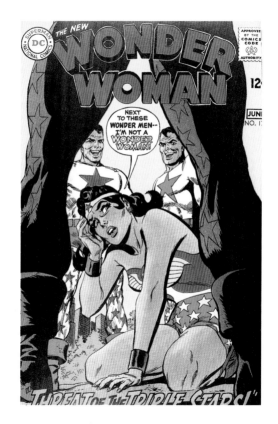

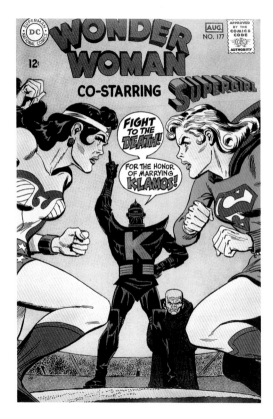

JULY-AUGUST 1968; NO. 177

Cover artist: Irv Novick

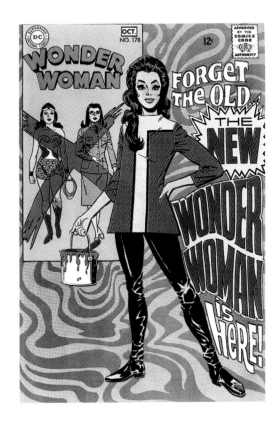

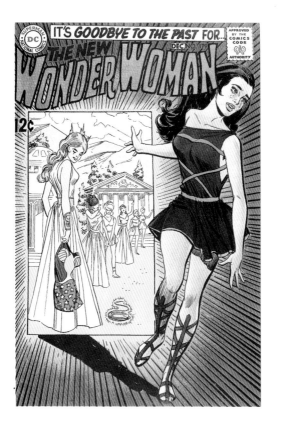

NOVEMBER–DECEMBER 1968; NO. 179

Cover artists: Mike Sekowsky, Dick Giordano

JANUARY-FEBRUARY 1969; NO. 180

Cover artists: Mike Sekowsky, Dick Giordano

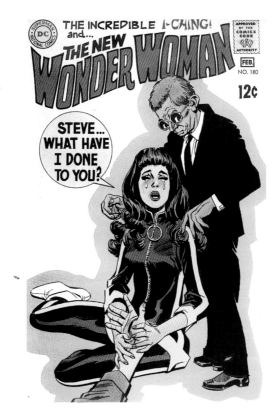

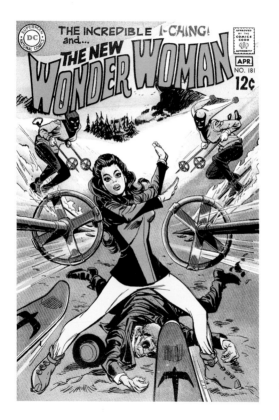

MARCH-APRIL 1969; NO. 181
· Cover artists: Mike Sekowsky, Dick Giordano

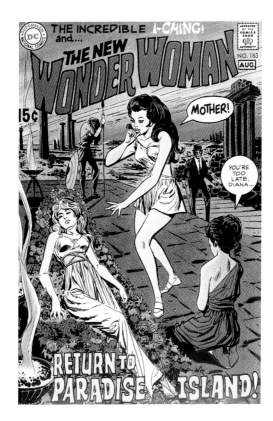

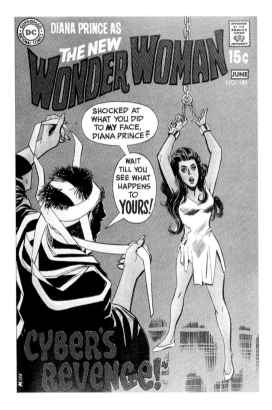

MAY–JUNE 1970; NO. 188

Cover artists: Mike Sekowsky, Dick Giordano

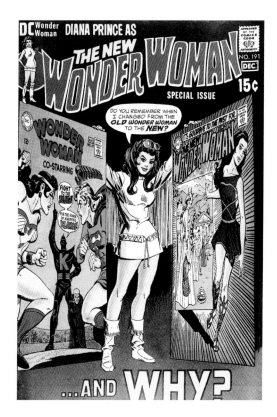

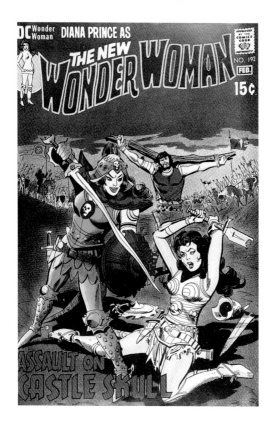

JANUARY-FEBRUARY 1971; NO. 192

Cover artists: Mike Sekowsky, Dick Giordano

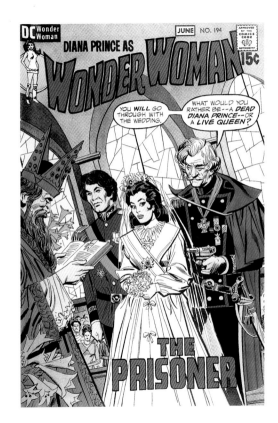

MAY–JUNE 1971; NO. 194
Cover artists: Mike Sekowsky, Dick Giordano

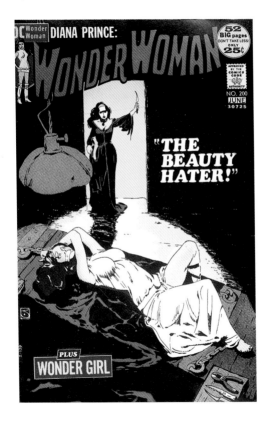

MAY–JUNE 1972; NO. 200
Cover artist: Jeff Jones

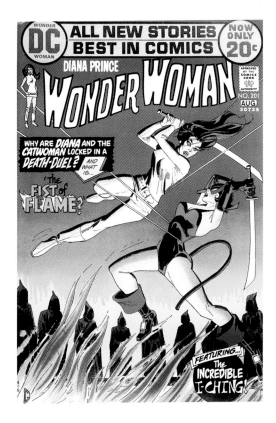

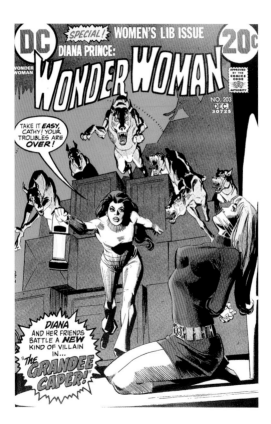

NOVEMBER–DECEMBER 1972; NO. 203

Cover artist: Dick Giordano

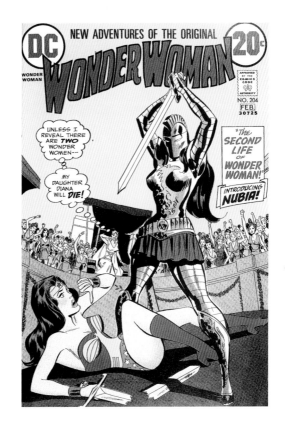

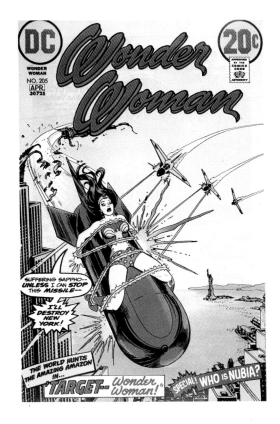

MARCH–APRIL 1973; NO. 205
Cover artist: Nick Cardy

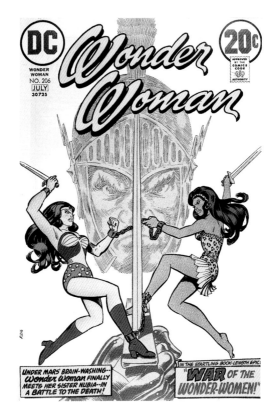

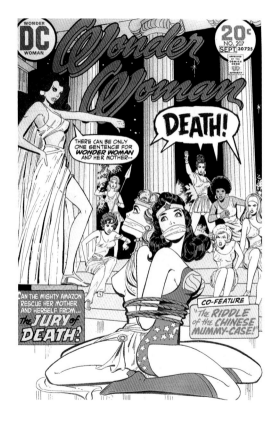

AUGUST–SEPTEMBER 1973; NO. 207
Cover artists: Ric Estrada, Vince Colletta

FEBRUARY–MARCH 1974; NO. 210
Cover artists: Ric Estrada, Vince Colletta

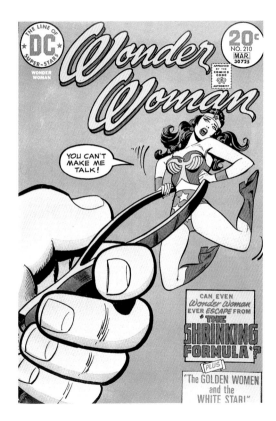

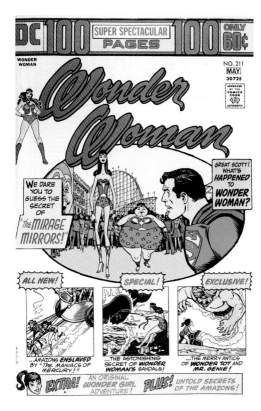

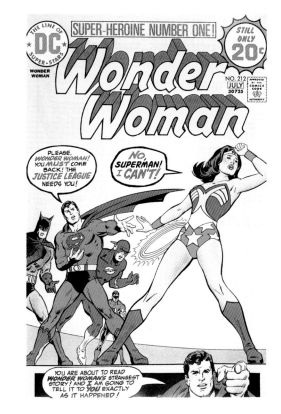

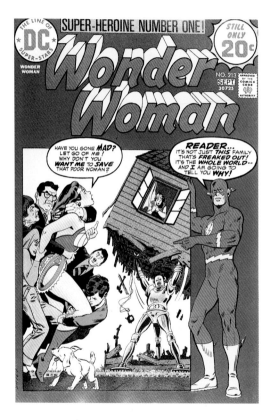

AUGUST-SEPTEMBER 1974; NO. 213

Cover artist: Bob Oksner

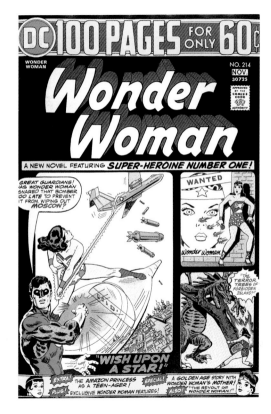

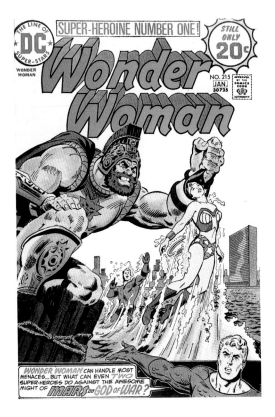

DECEMBER 1974–JANUARY 1975; NO. 215

Cover artist: Bob Oksner

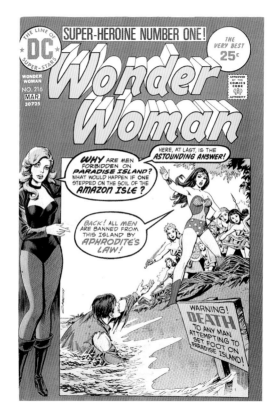

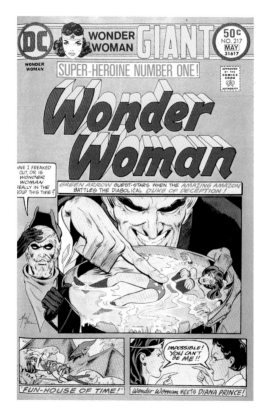

APRIL–MAY 1975; NO. 217
Cover artist: Mike Grell

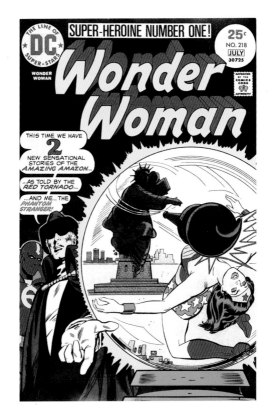

AUGUST–SEPTEMBER 1975; NO. 219

Cover artist: Dick Giordano

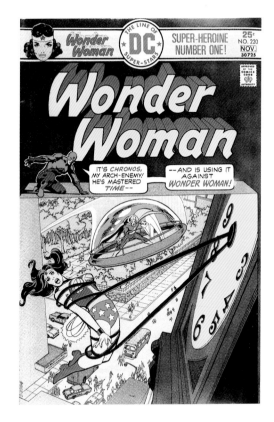

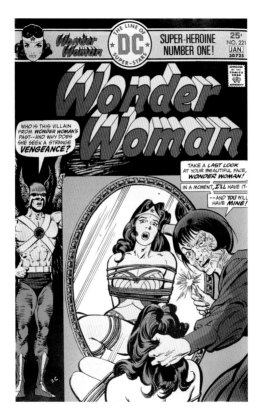

DECEMBER 1975–JANUARY 1976; NO. 221

Cover artist: Ernie Chan

FEBRUARY–MARCH 1976; NO. 222
Cover artist: Ernie Chan

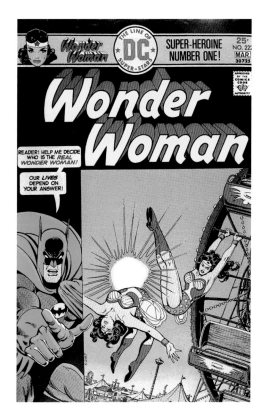

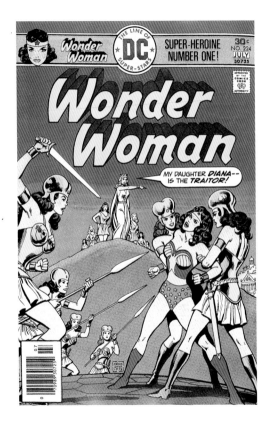

JUNE-JULY 1976; NO. 224

Cover artist: Ernie Chan

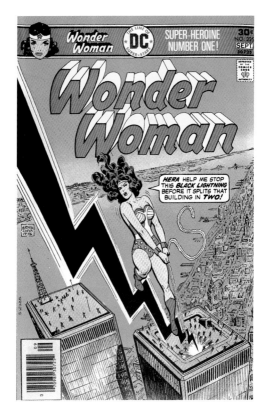

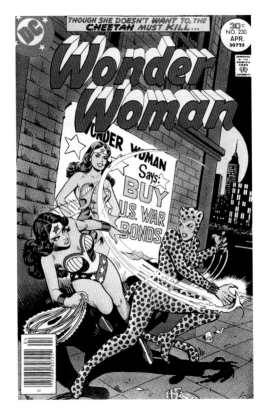

APRIL 1977; NO. 230
Cover artists: José Luis García-López, Vince Colletta

MAY 1977; NO. 231

Cover artists: Michael Nasser, Vince Colletta

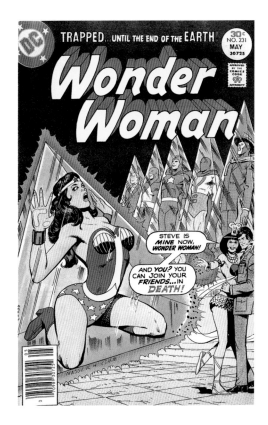

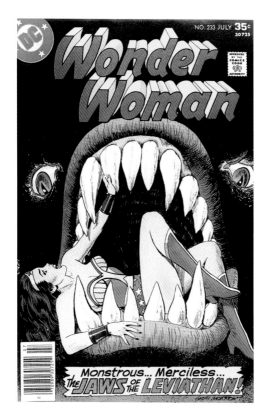

JULY 1977; NO. 233
Cover artist: Gray Morrow

NOVEMBER 1977; NO. 237
Cover artists: Rich Buckler, Vince Colletta

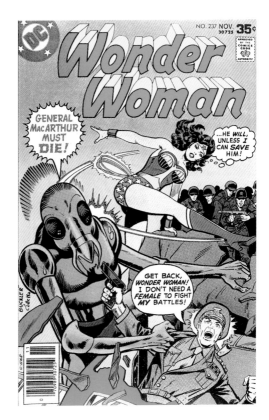

JANUARY 1978; NO. 239
Cover artists: Rich Buckler, Vince Colletta

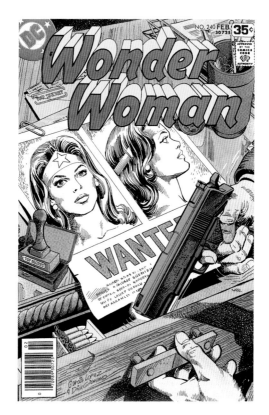

FEBRUARY 1978; NO. 240

Cover artists: José Luis Garcia-López, Dick Giordano

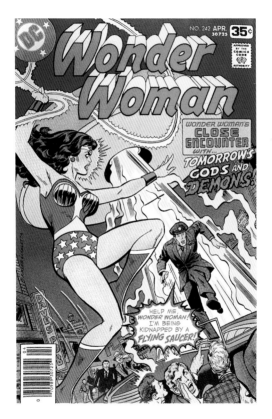

APRIL 1978: NO. 242

Cover artists: Rich Buckler, Vince Colletta

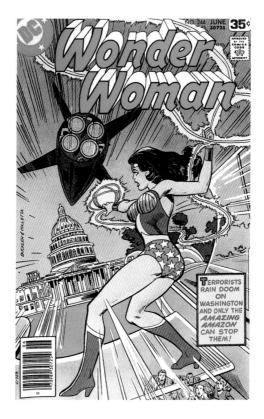

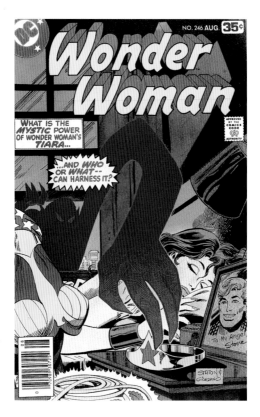

AUGUST 1978; NO. 246
Cover artists: Joe Staton, Dick Giordano

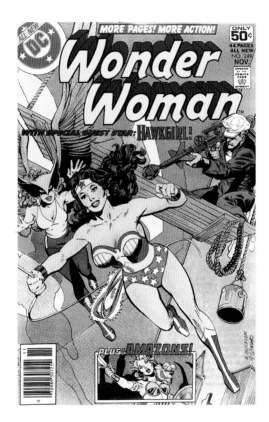

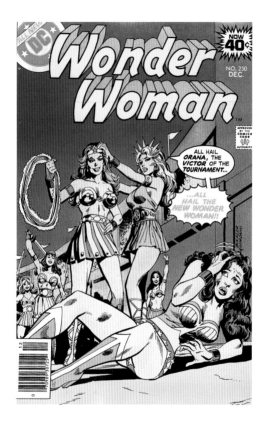

DECEMBER 1978; NO. 250
Cover artists: Rich Buckler, Dick Giordano

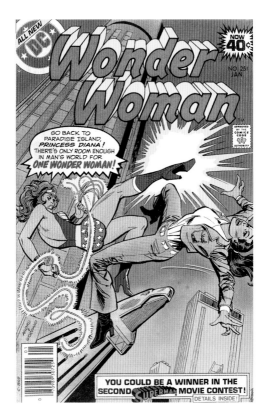

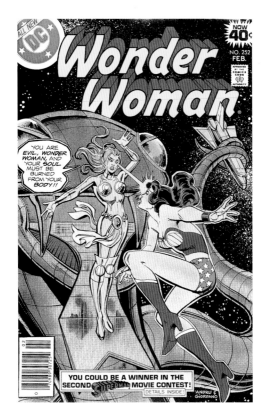

FEBRUARY 1979; NO. 252

Cover artists: Ross Andru, Dick Giordano

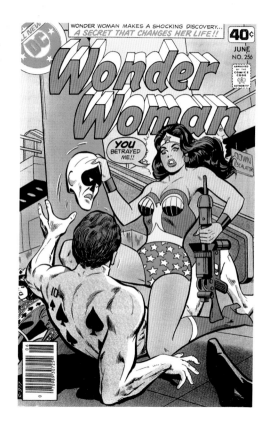

JUNE 1979; NO. 256
Cover artists: Jose Delbo, Vince Colletta

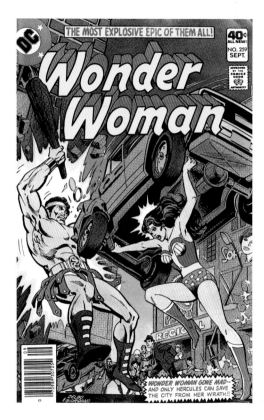

SEPTEMBER 1979; NO. 259
Cover artists: Jose Delbo, Vince Colletta

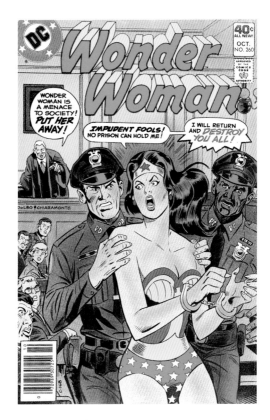

OCTOBER 1979; NO. 260
Cover artists: Jose Delbo, Frank Chiaramonte

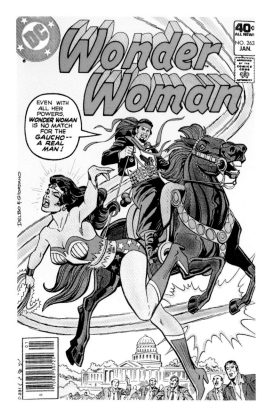

JANUARY 1980; NO. 263
Cover artists: Jose Delbo, Dick Giordano

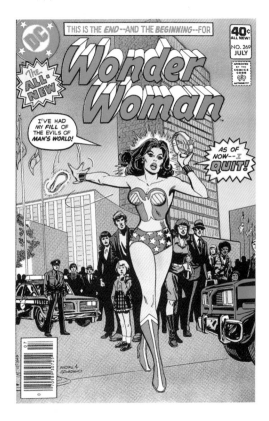

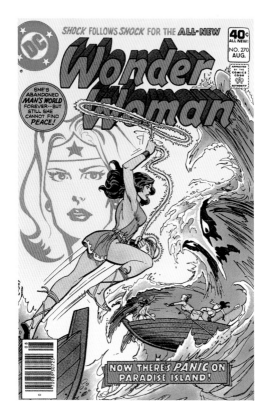

AUGUST 1980; NO. 270

Cover artists: Ross Andru, Dick Giordano

SEPTEMBER 1980; NO. 271
Cover artists: Ross Andru, Dick Giordano

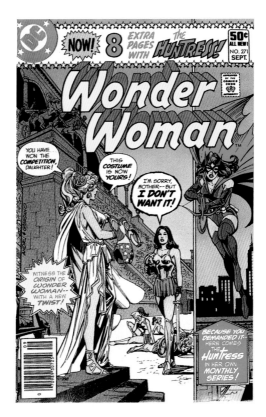

OCTOBER 1980; NO. 272
Cover artists: Dave Cockrum, Dick Giordano

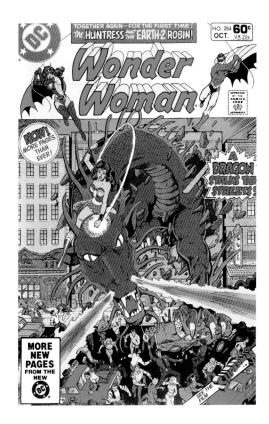

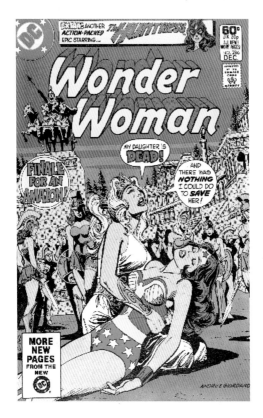

DECEMBER 1981; NO. 286
Cover artists: Ross Andru, Dick Giordano

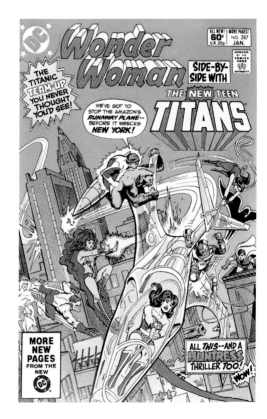

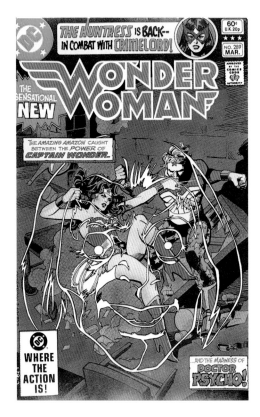

MARCH 1982; NO. 289

Cover artists: Gene Colan, Dick Giordano

SEPTEMBER 1982; NO. 295
Cover artists: Rich Buckler, Frank Giacoia

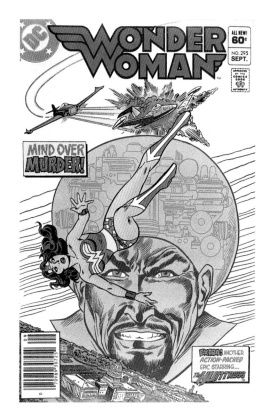

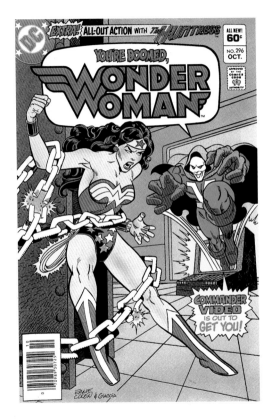

OCTOBER 1982; NO. 296

Cover artists: Ernie Colón, Frank Giacoia

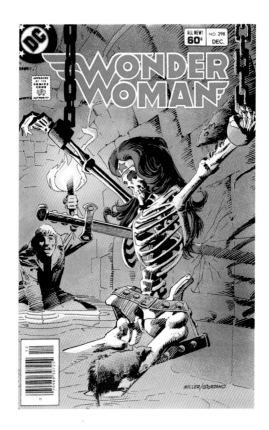

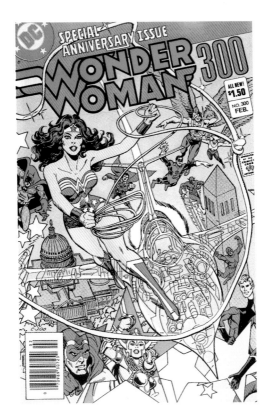

FEBRUARY 1983; NO. 300
Cover artists: Ed Hannigan, Dick Giordano

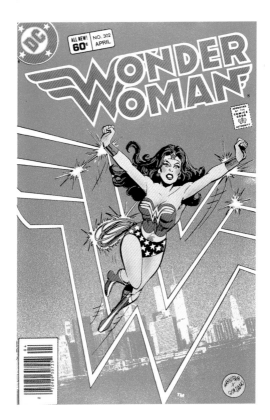

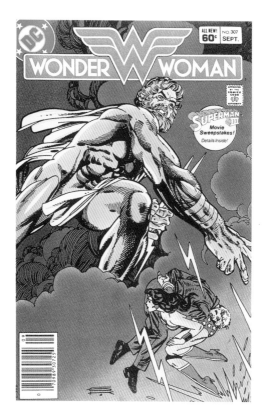

SEPTEMBER 1983; NO. 307

Cover artist: Gil Kane

OCTOBER 1983; NO. 308
Cover artists: Ross Andru, Dick Giordano

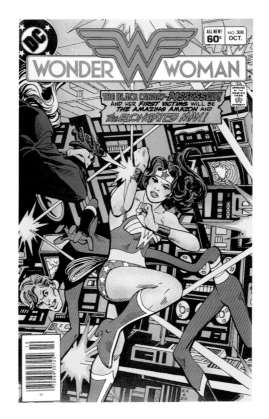

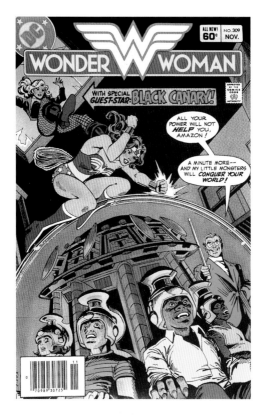

NOVEMBER 1983; NO. 309
Cover artists: Ross Andru, Dick Giordano

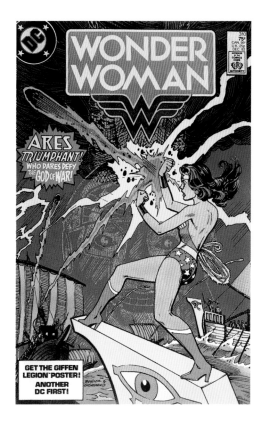

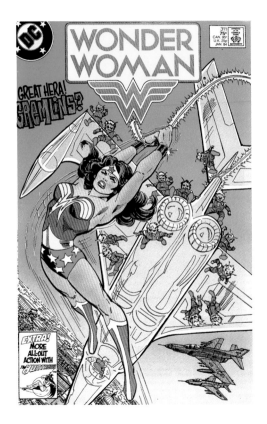

JANUARY 1984; NO. 311
Cover artists: Ross Andru, Dick Giordano

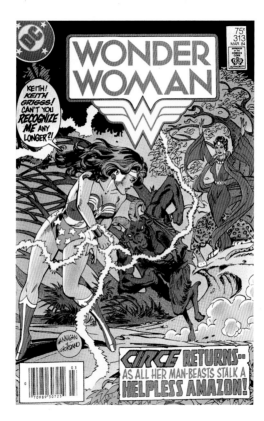

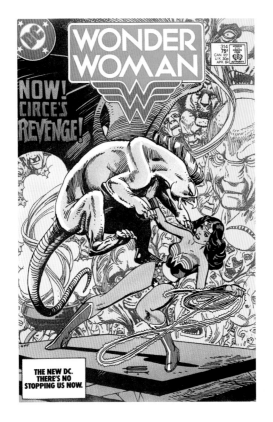

APRIL 1984; NO. 314
Cover artist: Gil Kane

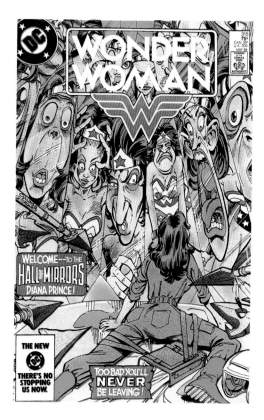

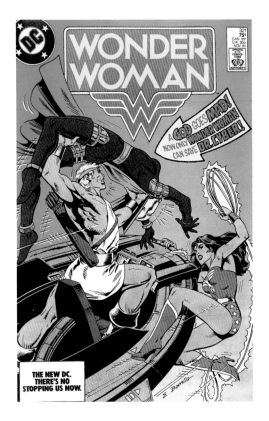

NOVEMBER 1984; NO. 321

Cover artist: Eduardo Barreto

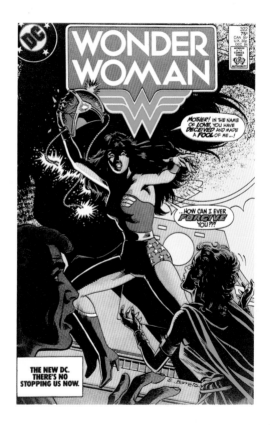

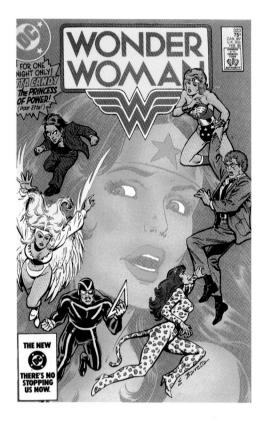

FEBRUARY 1985; NO. 323

Cover artist: Eduardo Barreto

SEPTEMBER 1985; NO. 327

Cover artist: Eduardo Barreto

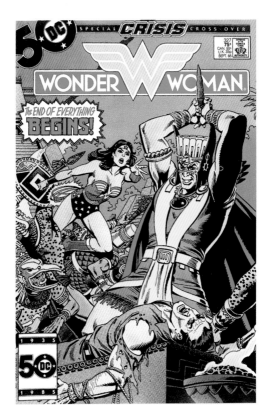

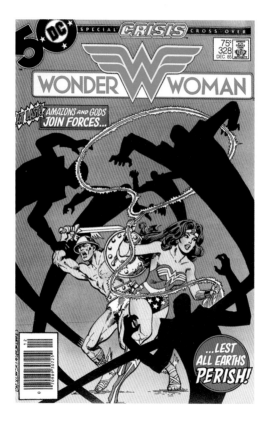

NOVEMBER 1985; NO. 328
Cover artist: Joe Brozowski, Dick Giordano

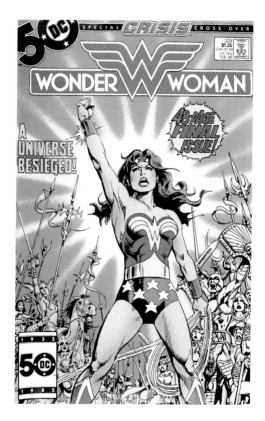

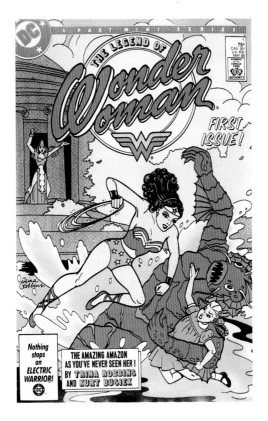

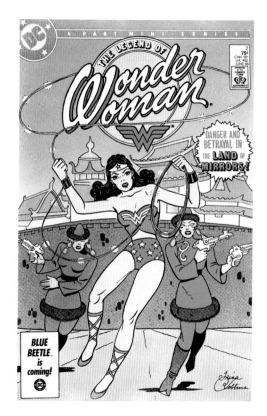

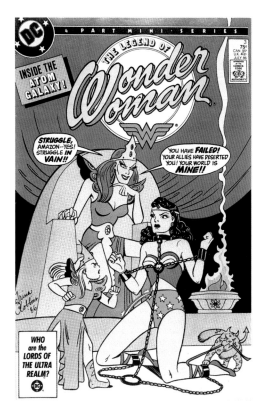

JULY 1986; NO. 3
Cover artist: Trina Robbins

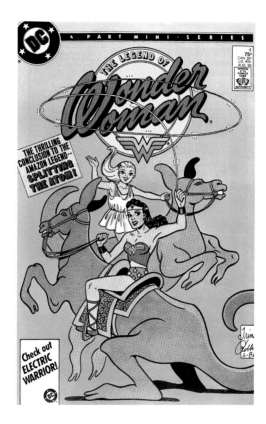

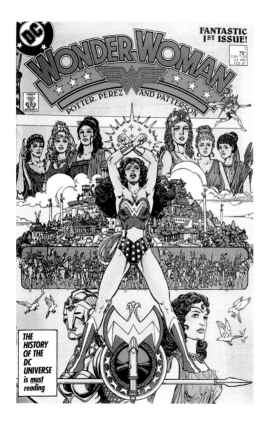

FEBRUARY 1987; NO. 1

Cover artist: George Pérez

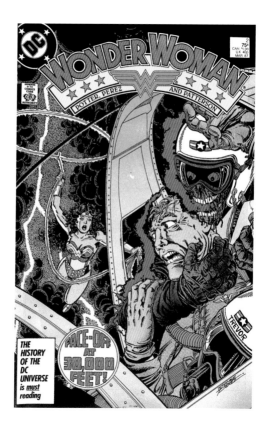

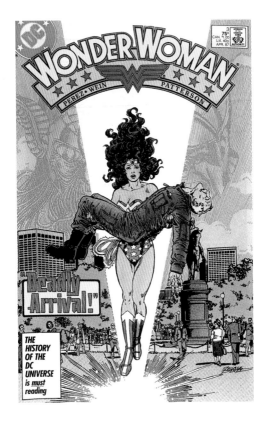

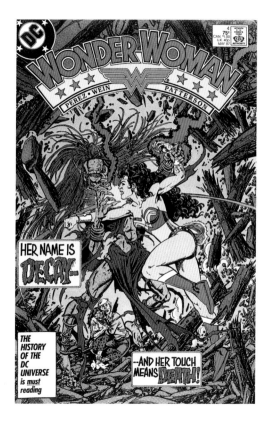

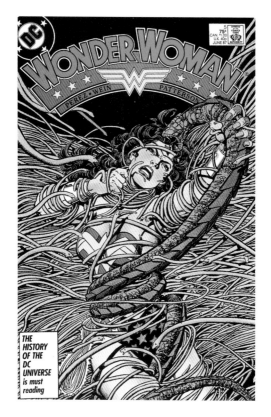

JUNE 1987; NO. 5
Cover artist: George Pérez

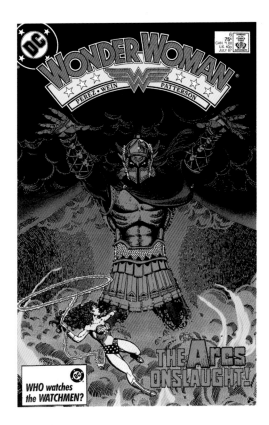

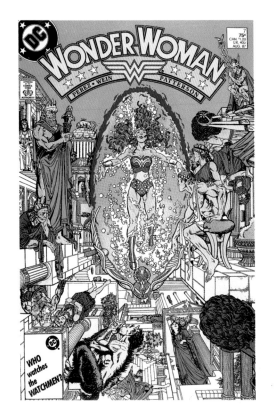

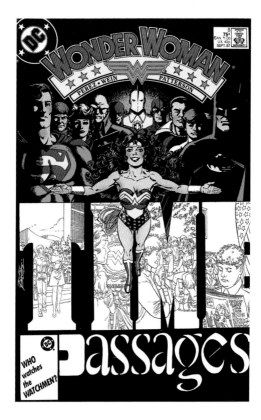

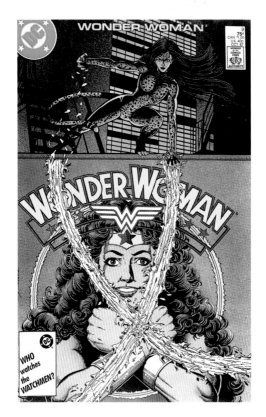

OCTOBER 1987; NO. 9
Cover artist: George Pérez

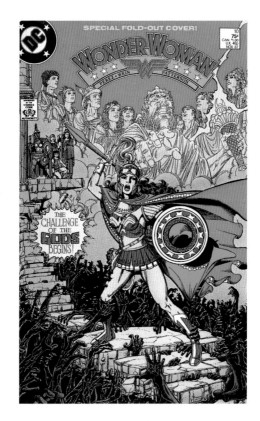

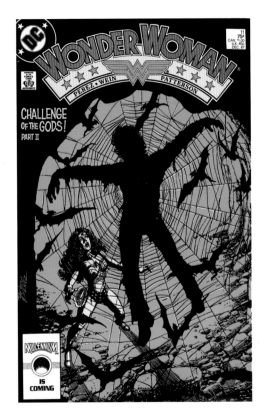

DECEMBER 1987; NO. 11
Cover artist: George Pérez

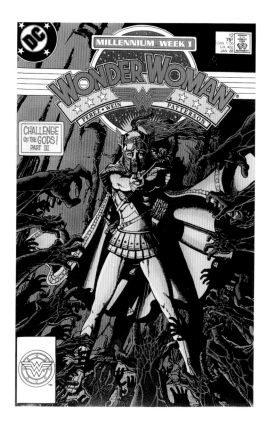

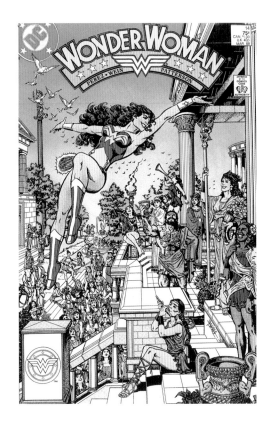

MARCH 1988; NO. 14
Cover artist: George Pérez

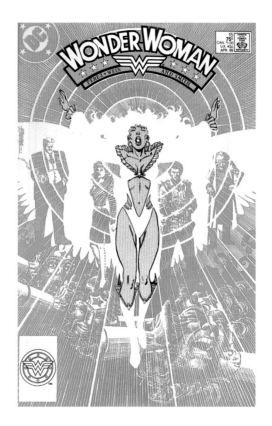

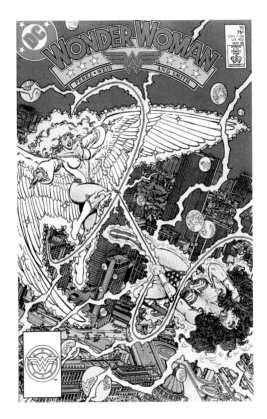

MAY 1988; NO. 16

Cover artist: George Pérez

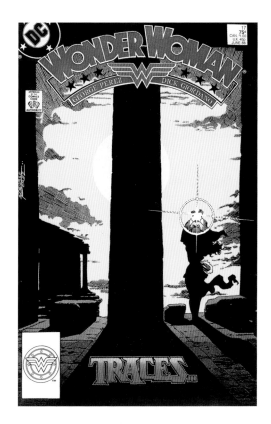

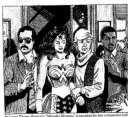
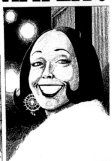

SEPTEMBER 1988; NO. 20
Cover artist: George Pérez

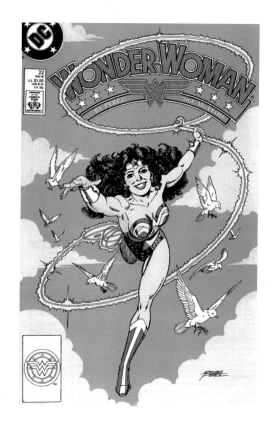

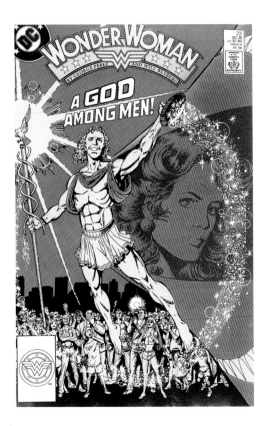

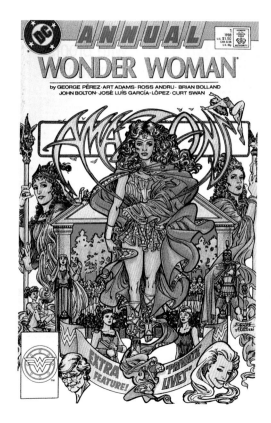

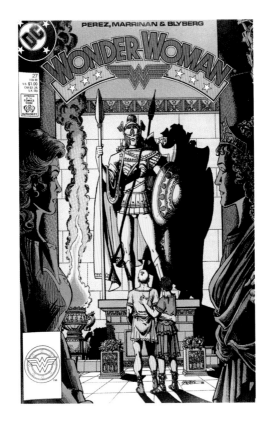

FEBRUARY 1989; NO. 27

Cover artist: George Pérez

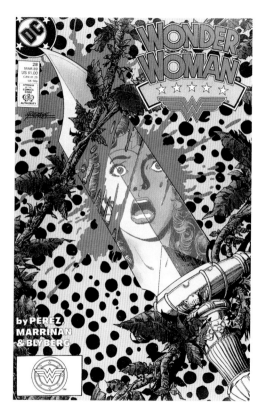

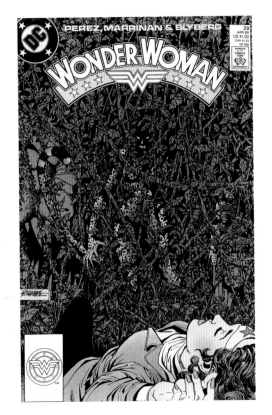

APRIL 1989; NO. 29

Cover artist: George Pérez

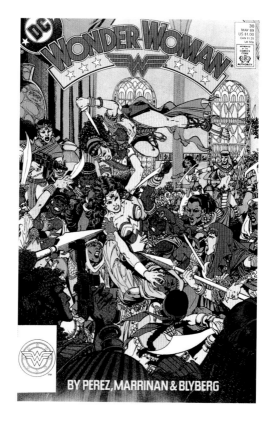

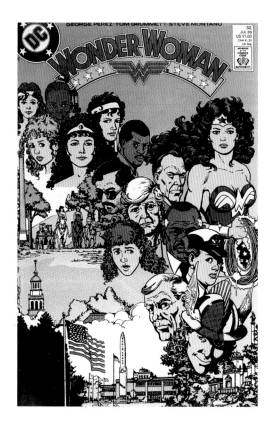

JULY 1989; NO. 32

Cover artist: George Pérez

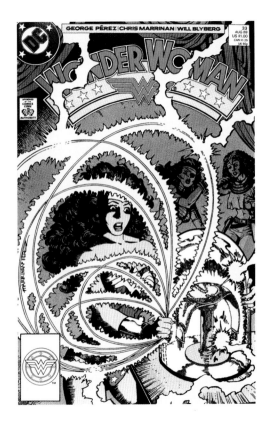

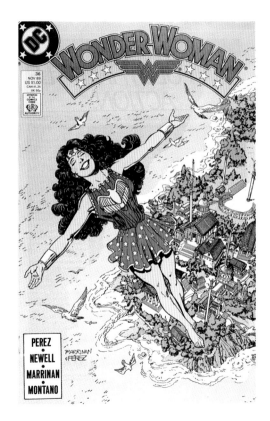

NOVEMBER 1989; NO. 36
Cover artists: Chris Marrinan, George Perez

JANUARY 1990; NO. 38
Cover artists: Chris Marrinan, George Pérez

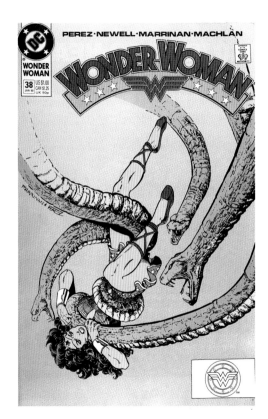

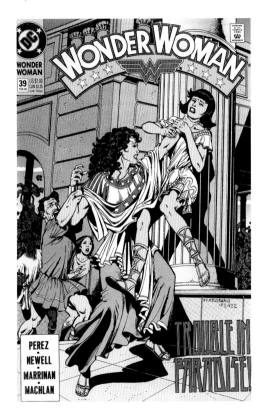

FEBRUARY 1990; NO. 39
Cover artists: Chris Marrinan, George Pérez

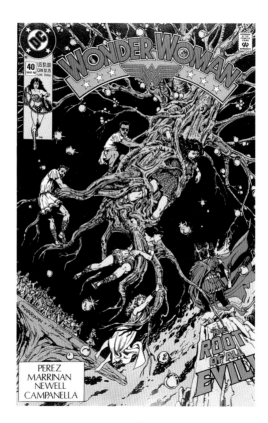

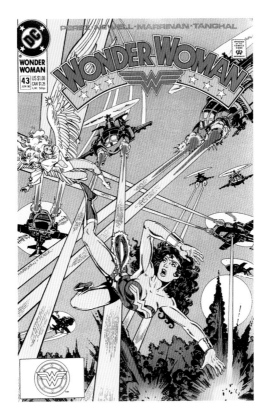

JUNE 1990; NO. 43

Cover artists: Chris Marrinan, George Pérez

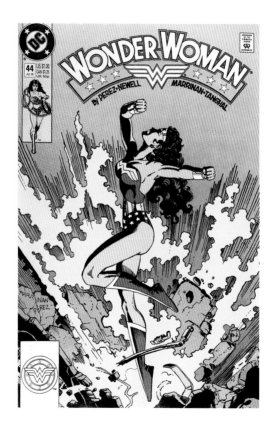

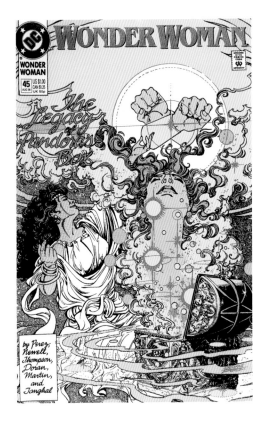

AUGUST 1990; NO. 45

Cover artists: George Pérez

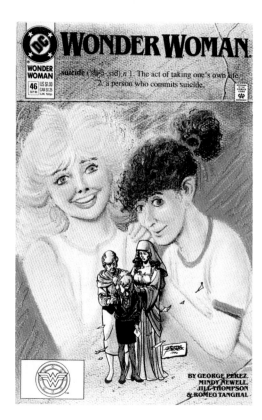

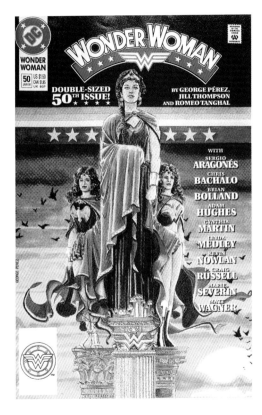

JANUARY 1991; NO. 50

Cover artist: George Pérez

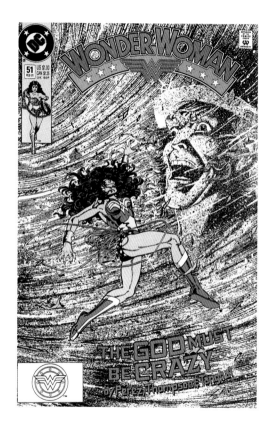

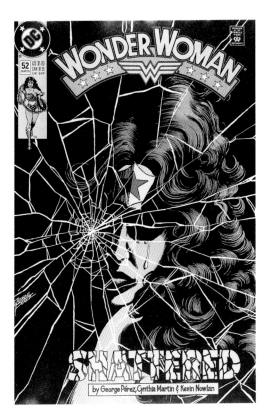

MARCH 1991; NO. 52

Cover artist: George Pérez

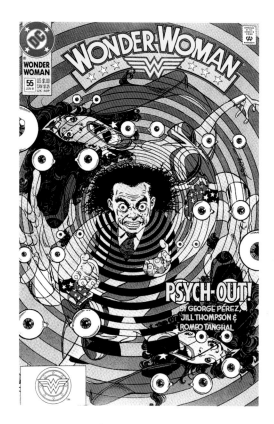

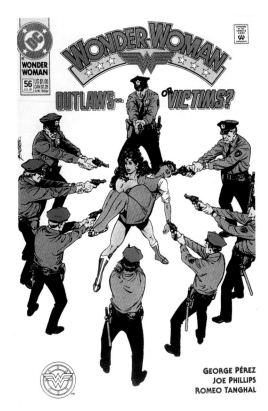

SEPTEMBER 1991; NO. 58
Cover artist: George Pérez

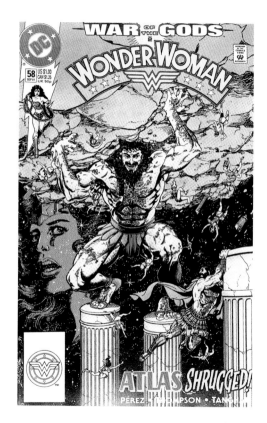

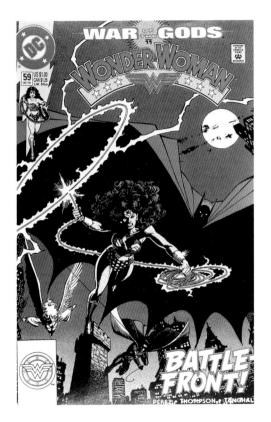

OCTOBER 1991; NO. 59

Cover artist: George Pérez

NOVEMBER 1991; NO. 60
Cover artist: George Pérez

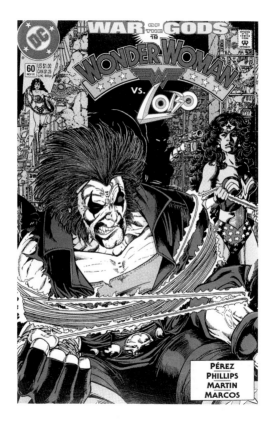

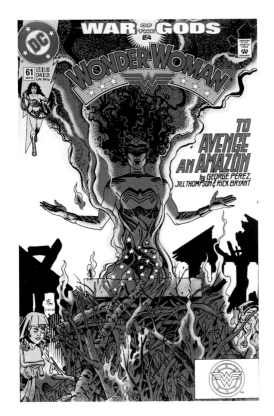

JANUARY 1992: NO. 61

Cover artists: Jill Thompson, Jay Geldhof

MAY 1992; NO. 1

Cover artists: Jill Thompson, Jerry Ordway

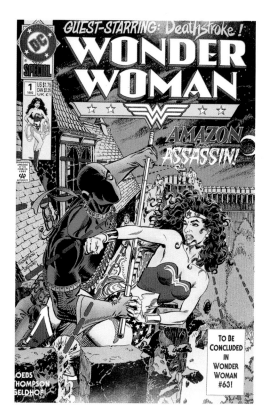

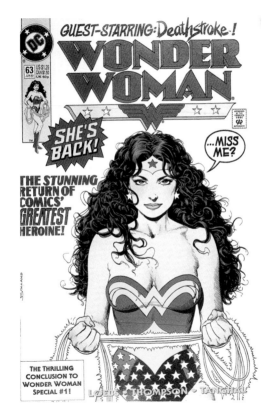

JUNE 1992; NO. 63
Cover artist: Brian Bolland

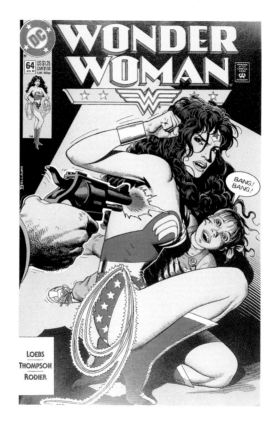

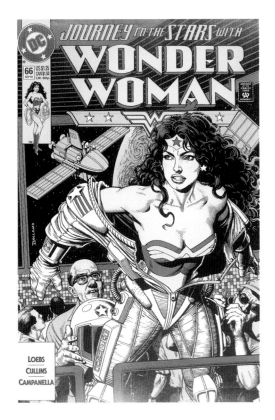

SEPTEMBER 1992; NO. 66

Cover artist: Brian Bolland

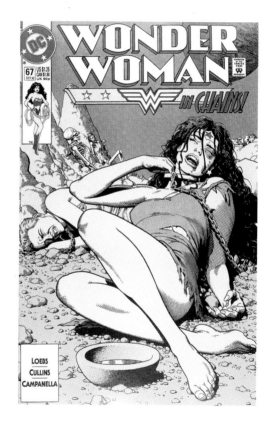

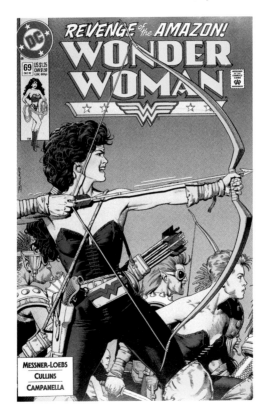

DECEMBER 1992; NO. 69

Cover artist: Brian Bolland

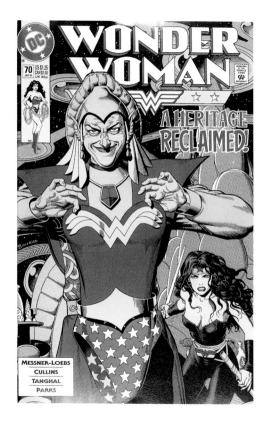

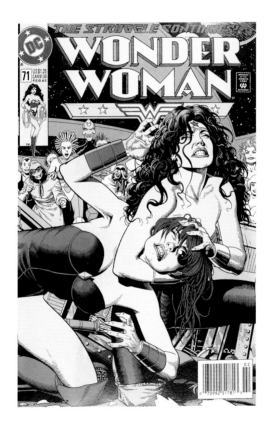

FEBRUARY 1993; NO. 71

Cover artist: Brian Bolland

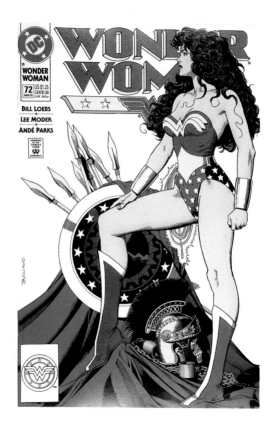

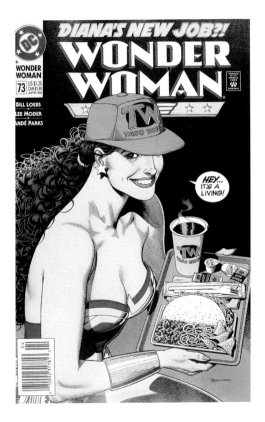

APRIL 1993; NO. 73

Cover artist: Brian Bolland

MAY 1993; NO. 74
Cover artist: Brian Bolland

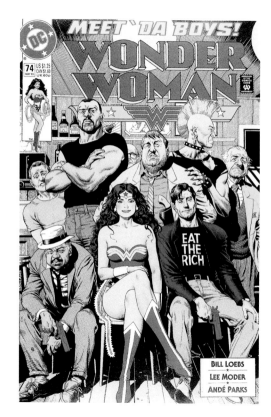

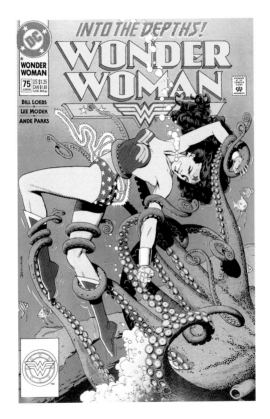

JUNE 1993; NO. 75

Cover artist: Brian Bolland

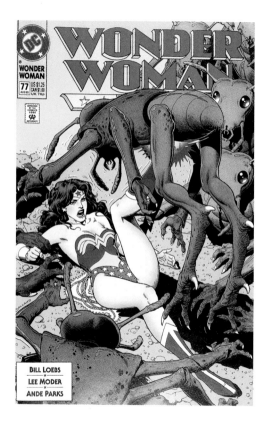

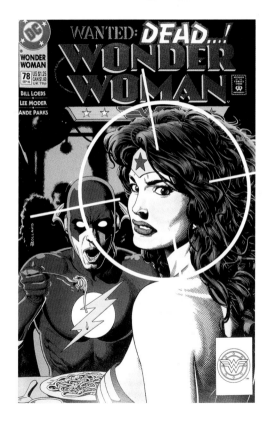

SEPTEMBER 1993; NO. 78

Cover artist: Brian Bolland

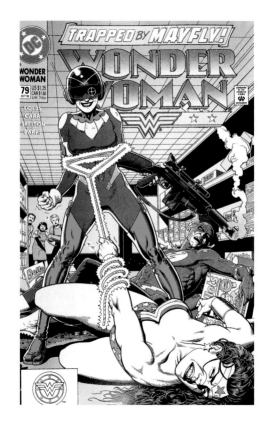

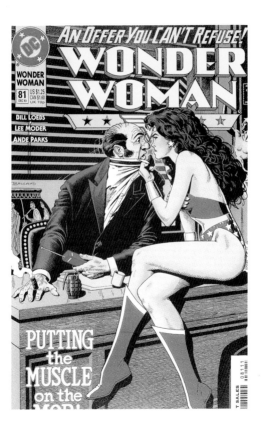

DECEMBER 1993; NO. 81
Cover artist: Brian Bolland

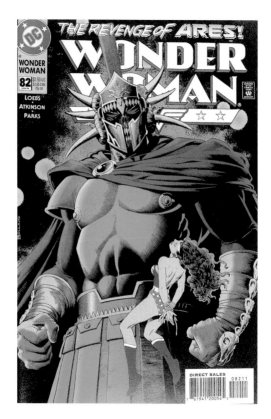

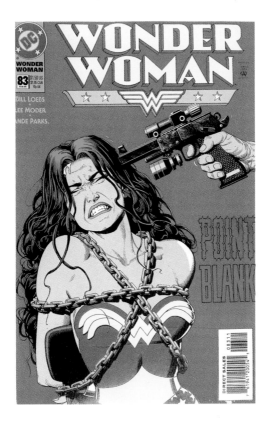

FEBRUARY 1994; NO. 83
Cover artist: Brian Bolland

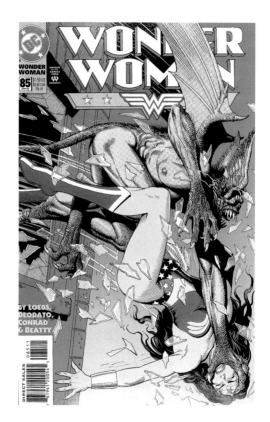

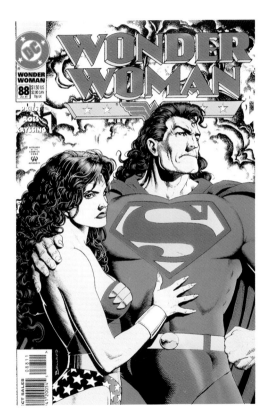

JULY 1994; NO. 88

Cover artist: Brian Bolland

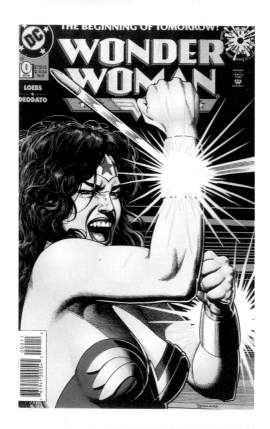